THE CITY BUILDERS

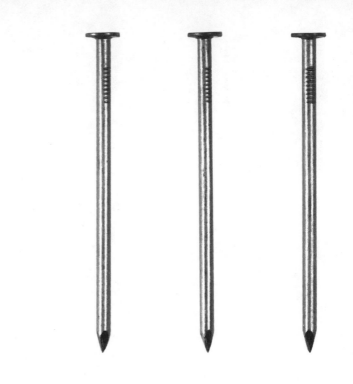

Oregon Historical Society Press

THE
CITY
BUILDERS

*One Hundred Years of
Union Carpentry
in Portland, Oregon
1883-1983*

CRAIG WOLLNER

The paper used in this publication meets the minimum requirements of American National Standard for Information Sciences—Permanence of Paper for Printed Library Materials, ANSI Z39.48-1984.

LIBRARY OF CONGRESS CATALOGING-IN-PUBLICATION DATA
Wollner, Craig, 1943-
    The city builders.
    Bibliography: p.
    1. United Brotherhood of Carpenters and Joiners of America—History. 2. Trade-unions—Carpenters—Oregon—Portland—History. I. Title.
HD6515.C2U59   1990   331.88'194'0979549   88-9914
ISBN 0-87595-198-8 (alk. paper) [infinity symbol]

Printed in the United States of America.

In memory of my father,
MACK S. WOLLNER,
and for my mother,
DOROTHY S. WOLLNER

CONTENTS

THE CITY BUILDERS

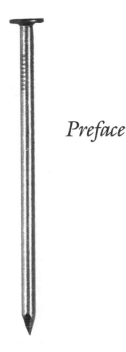

Preface

THE CARPENTERS' UNION OF PORTLAND, Oregon, chartered in 1883, has, as this is written, survived for more than one hundred years. Specifically, Local No. 247, a direct descendant of the original Portland Local No. 50 of the United Brotherhood of Carpenters and Joiners of America, celebrated its centennial in 1983 and still represents the economic, social, and political aspirations of over twenty-one hundred men and women who earn their livelihoods in one of the world's oldest and most honored crafts, much as its founders intended that it should.

A hundred years is a long time for anything to exist, particularly in the western United States, where a century ago there were few well-established institutions of any kind. In fact, the union is only twenty-four years younger than the state of Oregon and thirty-two years younger than the city of Portland. It has thus had the opportunity to play a decisive role in shaping Oregon's most important economic center, and therefore Oregon itself, almost from the beginnings of each. If this role has been little re-marked, one has only to note the city's constructed elements—its homes, offices, government buildings, libraries, hospitals, schools, roads, bridges, dams, ships, and docks—to understand its significance. For with their hands, the union carpenters of Portland created much of Portland.

The city's architectural development notwithstanding, the most fas-cinating aspect of the union's history is the interplay of the social, political, and economic forces that have buffeted organized labor in its relationship to its employers and its work over the last one hundred years. The carpen-ters' union has had to respond and adapt to numerous recessions, the Great Depression, two world wars, and the changing attitudes of elected officials and the general public toward its goals. Moreover, it has had to develop an appreciation of the rapidly moving imperatives of technology. Changes in the methods of the construction industry have inevitably in-volved transformations in the nature of carpentry. If carpentry has changed, that, in turn, has affected the relationship of the union with other building trades, sometimes raising critical questions of jurisdiction at the jobsite. Over the years such instances, coupled with the management's requirements, have led to various confrontations of the carpenters with their employers. Intrinsically connected to these broad developments has been the fate of thousands of individual workers, the husbanding of whose energies and dignity is the union's ultimate responsibility. This fundamen-tal aspect of the carpenters' union's existence in Portland is what gives its century-long story its resonance.

This essay, then, is about the task the founders of Local No. 50 under-took in 1883: to honor and safeguard the integrity of their craft, to promote the welfare of their fellow workers, to participate in the building of a major American city, and to make their collective voice heard in the chambers of power whenever the future of the city and its inhabitants was being shaped.

In telling this story, I have adhered to a few principles that need to be stated at the outset. First, I have tried to focus less on internecine union politics and more on the interaction of social, political, and economic forces and the Portland carpenter locals as a whole. This is because the internal dynamics of the carpenters' union have been more than adequately studied by Walter Galenson in his book *The United Brotherhood of Carpenters: The First Hundred Years* and by Thomas R. Brooks in *The Road to Dignity: A Century of Conflict*. While these works are clearly about the union on a national scale, they leave little doubt as to the specific impacts of union politics on individual locals. For the most part, to have delved more deeply into many of these matters would, I believe, have produced a highly specialized essay of limited appeal, even among union members. At the same time, I have eschewed what has come to be called the "new labor history," with its emphasis on such issues as gender, race, class, religion, and family dynamics among its working-class subjects. Such a focus would surely have been revealing to scholars, but again would have restricted my audience to those with a more technical interest in unions and their history.

The second principle of this work flows from the first. In choosing this focus, I have frequently sacrificed individual identities in pursuing the fullest possible understanding of the larger processes that have shaped the union's activities in Portland. This may annoy some who expect from such exercises a more personal form of storytelling, and alarm others who will protest that the essay lacks a human dimension.

To such critics, I can only say that at all times in researching and writing this work, I have retained the sense that the story of the carpenters' union in Portland is the story of real men and women, bound up in the patterns of history. I can only hope that my sensitivity to this truth is apparent in my prose.

The third principle guiding me has been that this should be a work of public, or—as it is sometimes called—applied, history. By this I mean work that must above all meet every standard of scholarly research and critical thinking implicit in the traditional historical enterprise. Such a work also attempts not only to add to the store of human knowledge, but to present itself as a tool of some more immediate and explicit end.

When this essay was commissioned, it seemed clear to me that the union—ironically, at the very moment of observing its longevity—was in crisis. Hard times and crucial shifts in American attitudes toward organized labor and in the technology of construction had demoralized the union, depleted its ranks, and put it on the defensive. It occurred to me that the history I wrote should point plainly and boldly to the specific developments and broad configurations that brought the union carpenters of Portland to the pass at which they found themselves in 1983. I considered that the historical perspective would be useful to the union, and would provide a "public" purpose to the essay, as a map of the past that might indicate a route to the future. This view strengthened my resolve to hew to the tenets I have already discussed. In addition, I felt it necessary to explore the union's activities since World War II and the circumstances surrounding them, as the events of those years were the most obvious sources of the carpenters' situation in 1983. Consequently, I have given somewhat disproportionate attention to a period many historians feel is, properly speaking, not yet quite "history."

While the success of this self-assigned task is for others to judge, I would like to say what a worthwhile and fulfilling undertaking it was for me. This was partly because I was always made to feel by those associated with the union that what I was doing was significant to the organization. It was also because I was always encouraged by every carpenter I encountered to find and write only the truth, a fact that I hope shines through on each page of this work.

Acknowledgments

BEGUN AS THE BRAINCHILD OF LEO LAR-
sen, of Carpenters' Local No. 226, *The City Builders* was
written to commemorate the union's centennial in Port-
land in 1983. Eventually the original fifty-page essay grew to the size of the
present work.

In the largest measure, my satisfaction in writing this work is due to
the assistance of the many persons with whom I was associated in its
course. The members of the centennial committee of Local No. 247, including George Edwards, Mike Fitzpatrick, Kate Barrett, Phil Loiodici,
Rick Adams, Ed Stange, Steven Taylor, and Boyd Kinnan, were a constant
source of support and encouragement. The office staff of 247, Betty Clin-
ton, Jeri Butcher, Diane Whitehead, and Linda Van Denderen, were always helpful in addressing my endless requests for information or aid of
one kind or another. Toni Linné, of the office staff of the State District
Council of Carpenters, was similarly responsive to my numerous queries.

Jim Fox, research director of the State District Council, also provided answers to many questions and a guiding hand when needed information was not at his fingertips. At the headquarters of the United Brotherhood of Carpenters in Washington, D.C., Elizabeth Kent and Theresa Threlfall were much more than merely helpful during my brief visit there, and they continued their assistance after I had left by extending the same kindness to my friend Michael Musillo, whom I asked to complete some unfinished tasks. To Michael, and to Cynthia Musillo, I owe a debt of gratitude that may simply be added to my ever-open account. Mark Furman, Harry Carlson, Dudley Franco, and all the other informants listed in the bibliography were of crucial importance to this undertaking.

John Leffler, Patrick Harris, and Ellen Payne provided invaluable research and proofreading skills in the preparation of this manuscript, while Shirley Heidinger proved to be a splendid typist. The knowledge, wisdom, and common sense of such colleagues at Portland State University as Gordon Dodds, a titan among historians of the Pacific Northwest; David Johnson, whose grasp of social history and critical eye were important resources; and Jim Heath, a veritable encyclopedia of modern American history, were essential to me. Bernard V. Burke and Frederick M. Nunn have always been sources of inspiration in matters of scholarship and continued to serve that function during the writing of this essay. Ralph Wiser's knowledge of labor law and his friendship were of great assistance, as were the insight and sagacity of John Rosenberg.

Finally, tribute must be paid to the courage, vision, patience, kindness, and loyalty of one who was indispensable to this project. Leo Larsen, financial secretary of Local No. 247, insisted on the importance to his membership of this history and, amidst criticism, won their permission to have it completed. The resulting study stems directly from his determination that it be done, that it be the best and most honest portrayal it could be, and that it be a real contribution to historical knowledge. His understanding and encouragement were vital to its completion. In short, without Leo Larsen this history could not have been undertaken.

While the many hands and minds of those noted above share the honor of any success this essay may meet, I alone am responsible for its interpretations of fact and for errors of any kind that may appear in its pages.

THE CITY BUILDERS

ONE
Beginnings

IN 1883 PORTLAND, OREGON, WAS A CITY
with a population of approximately twenty-one thousand five hundred.[1] It bustled with the energy typical of a
young and ambitious western metropolis. Its burgeoning local economy,
based on lumber, salmon, and grain, was accommodated by the completion on 8 September of the transcontinental rail line, the Northern Pacific.
This, with its highway to the Pacific, the Columbia River, made Portland
the natural market center for the vast hinterland of eastern Oregon, Washington, and Idaho.

The city's physical growth was impressive. Employment levels rose as
jobs became more plentiful in the last two decades of the nineteenth century. Widespread prosperity in the new land seemed inevitable. But in Portland, as throughout the United States, the development of a sophisticated
market economy and industrial society engendered problems. If more jobs
were available, they could be secured only at low wages. Long hours,

unsafe and unhealthy working conditions, and other social and economic injustices were also part of the new economic growth.[2]

These conditions had been created at the end of the Civil War—a war that had been fought as much over whether to turn the nation into the industrialized society that northern businessmen envisioned or to preserve its agrarian character as southerners desired, as over the more explosive issue of slavery. In the war's aftermath, the triumphant proponents of industrialization started a veritable revolution in the nation's economic order that gave free rein to ruthless entrepreneurs—the so-called captains of industry—such as John D. Rockefeller, "Big" Jim Fiske, and Cornelius Vanderbilt.

In the absence of government regulation over wages, hours, and health and safety in the workplace, as well as business competition in general, the industrial barons used human beings as tools to gain every competitive advantage. In so doing, they created a modern economy, but not a modern society.

Farmers, laborers, and members of the middle class, however, soon responded to the challenge of industrialization and its inequities with a variety of political and economic reform movements and organizations. Beginning in the 1870s, with the Grange movement and, later, the Populist party, the agrarians of the Midwest and the South lashed out against the power of the corporations, particularly the railroads. After the Civil War, middle-class reformism began feebly with the revolt of the Mugwumps in the presidential election of 1884, when normally Republican, small-town professionals turned their backs on the Grand Old Party (by then almost exclusively the creature of big business) and its candidate, James G. Blaine, in favor of the reform Democrat, Grover Cleveland.

The Mugwumps (their "mugs" on one side of the fence and their "wumps" on the other) subsided after the election, but their reformist spark helped ignite the growing social and political movement that became known as Progressivism. Decidedly middle class but more inclusive than Mugwumpery, Progressivism grew in power and scope to become a primary vehicle of protest against social and economic injustice through the first half of the twentieth century.

Throughout much of the nineteenth century, the American laboring classes were mixed in their attitudes toward unions and collective bargaining. In the early part of the century, skilled craftsmen as well as common laborers and recently arrived immigrants clung to their vision of individual social and economic mobility, as if submerging themselves in a larger interest group would limit their freedom and cut them off from the American Dream. Even with the inequities of the postwar revolution, American workers were, on the whole, slow to accept unions as the answer to their problems. Over the course of the century, perhaps 10 percent of industrial workers were unionized. In the total labor force, 2 percent, at most, belonged to unions.

However, several organizations dedicated to the betterment of labor were born. In 1866, William Sylvis of Pennsylvania formed the National Labor Union, in an effort to unite existing trade unions under one banner. Except for promoting the eight-hour day and safeguarding the status of craftsmen, though, the National Labor Union's agenda was a melange of ideals only peripherally related to the urgent concerns of workers. The organization, which eschewed the strike as a tool, tried to effect change through a political arm known as the National Labor Reform party. In 1872, the party failed at the polls and disappeared.

The Noble and Holy Order of the Knights of Labor, founded in 1869, sought to organize all workers—white, black, skilled, and unskilled—into one monolithic union, as a means of combating "the aggression of employers." Their platform included the eight-hour day, abolition of child and convict labor, arbitration of disputes rather than the use of the strike, and consumer and producer cooperative stores and factories. The Knights, under the leadership of Terence V. Powderly, their grand master workman, waxed and waned in strength and influence throughout the '70s and '80s, only to fade into oblivion by 1890. Their decline stemmed largely from their association in the public mind—unfairly, as it happened—with violence such as the Haymarket Riot of 4 May 1886 in Chicago.

Even as Powderly and the Knights of Labor went into eclipse, Samuel Gompers and the American Federation of Labor (AFL), formed in 1881, were marching to the forefront of the labor movement. Where Powderly and the Knights tended toward the romantic and idealistic in their methods and objectives, Gompers and the AFL sought to improve the condition of workers through a simple and practical program founded on a straight-forward plan of action. The AFL's goals were higher wages, shorter hours, and better working conditions. Powderly's plan for one huge union con-trasted with Gompers's strategy of trade unionism, with workers first or-ganizing within individual crafts. These groups of highly skilled craftsmen would work for their own economic betterment by addressing needs spe-cific to their own industries. The individual craft unions would have the power to call their own strikes. The AFL would act as a coordinating body, mediating jurisdictional problems among unions and linking local unions to one another through AFL-controlled state and national federations.

One union of the kind Gompers wanted was the United Brotherhood of Carpenters and Joiners. Also founded in 1881, the Carpenters' Union was made up of proud and independent men who considered themselves princes among craftsmen. Their vocation was an ancient one, requiring an immense store of knowledge and experience for skillful practice. A sense of the pride journeymen carpenters took in their craft and the status it con-ferred on them as independent craftsmen is gained from late-nineteenth-century photographs, which show them posing on buildings under con-struction. They wear stiff collars and cravats under their work clothes. At the end of the day, they removed their overalls and strode away from the job in suits and fedoras, the equals of the boss.

The man most responsible for the early success of the United Brother-hood was its first general secretary, Peter J. McGuire. A superb organizer, brilliant orator and able social critic, McGuire held socialist views. He was also a pragmatist who understood and was prepared to deal with the press-ing problems of his craft under the new American industrial order.

A bulletin issued by the U.S. Bureau of Labor in 1888 encapsulates the concerns McGuire identified.

> Many are the architectural changes year after year that are making
> carpenters work more and more scarce. The use of iron and steel and
> other material to replace wood; the general use of the best perfected
> woodworking machinery and of cheap mill material made by women
> and children; the lack of an apprentice system and the easy influx of
> workmen from other occupations into the carpenter trade.[3]

Modernization was tearing apart the ancient rhythms and order of carpentry. A project that had always been a seamless flow of complex operations undertaken only by a well-trained hand became a series of simple, discrete, and repetitive tasks, requiring less and less carpentry and more and more machine work. For example, new planing machines could prepare one thousand feet of oak flooring in twenty-three minutes—a job that would have required one hundred and ten man-hours of tonguing, grooving, and beading.[4]

The fragmentation of the carpenter's craft, and the diminution of the skills necessary to practice it, in turn weakened its wage-and-hour structure. For centuries carpentry had been undertaken as daywork, as the exercise of the craft, husbanded by a necessarily small group, could be compensated only on the basis of a large unit of time. A carpenter's labor was thus protected from devaluation. However, the linking of carpentry to the economics of mass production, and the admission of a flood of specialists (floor layers, stair builders, and so on) and machine operators to the craft, created the conditions of piecework and rapidly undermined wages. In such a situation, neither the hand carpenter nor the machine operator was fairly compensated.[5]

The journeyman was caught in a double bind. In 1880 in Washington, D.C., when wages were ostensibly two dollars per day, the carpenter who engaged in piecework probably earned about $1.00. Yet on the day-scale in the fall, when the working day grew shorter as darkness arrived earlier, he probably worked only 75 percent of a full day and earned $1.50. With a long apprenticeship, the responsibility for buying expensive tools, the constant threat of on-the-job injury, and the seasonal nature of the construction business, which nonetheless continued in the most inclement weather, the carpenter was working not toward the American Dream, but toward wage slavery.

McGuire outlined his solution to the craft's distress in the first issue of the new union's official organ, *The Carpenter*:

> There is no hope for workingmen outside of organization. Without a trade union, the workman meets the employer at great disadvantage. The capitalist has the advantage of past accumulation; the

laborer, unassisted by combination, has not. Knowing this, the capitalist can wait, while his men, without funds, have no other alternative but to submit. But with organization the case is altered; and the more wide-spread the organization, the better. Then the workingman is able to meet the employer on equal terms. No longer helpless and without resources, he has not only his union treasury, but the moneys of sister unions to support him in his ventures.[6]

American carpenters had always had organizations of one kind or another—benevolent societies, protective associations, and so forth—that were weak or strong, depending on such things as locale, economic conditions, and numbers of carpenters in the vicinity. McGuire's call for a national labor union met a strong response in 1880 because these local organizations found themselves increasingly powerless to defend their members against their employers and the modern age generally. Furthermore, nearly a decade of softness in the economy, touched off by the financial panic of 1873, had depressed the construction industry, leaving many carpenters chronically unemployed and their local organizations consequently weakened.

During the boom that began in the 1880s, these organizations were larger but not more powerful. They were, however, more militant, not only because of their increasing frustration, but because of the immigration of large numbers of European craftsmen with a tradition of labor activism. Of the 373,143 persons identified as carpenters in the census of 1880, approximately 100,000 were not American natives.[7] But they remained proud and independent. McGuire's vision of the union, summed up in his phrase "simplicity of organization, autonomy of function, and federation of interests," promised local control over local union matters, with the resources of a national organization in reserve. This appealed to men who felt capable of administering their own affairs, yet recognized the need of a national power base to attain their goals.

It was no coincidence that McGuire's blueprint for the United Brotherhood of Carpenters and Joiners coincided with Samuel Gompers's vision of the purpose and functioning of craft unions within the AFL. McGuire had been Gompers's disciple since the two men had met in McGuire's student days. Together, they reflected the reform that was to affect every aspect of American life in the last decades of the century.

In Portland, adjustment to the new economic and social order was no less real or compelling than in the more populous East. In the decade of the 1870s, printers, typesetters, and longshoremen had organized the city's first local unions.[8]

In January 1878, the Workingman's Club, intended as a vehicle of political discussion and activity for the laboring class, was formed. While the club's platform was not universally supported by workingmen and actually caused dissension in their ranks, its planks are a good index of the issues of the day for labor. The most controversial endorsements were for greenbacks, a paper currency issued after the Civil War and favored by farmers and workers because its inflationary effect might increase their spending power; abolition of national banks, which had a deflationary effect on the money supply; and exclusion of the Chinese, whose immigration was seen as a threat by westerners because of their acceptance of low wages, long hours, and poor working conditions.

The Workingman's Club supported the successful campaign of the incumbent, William W. Thayer, for governor in 1878. Meanwhile, issues of particular concern to workers were discussed in short-lived newspapers such as the *Labor Gazette* of 1878 and *Labor World*.

In 1880, Portland seemed promising territory for the national ambitions of the Knights of Labor. The Knights sent James Sovereign, who later succeeded Powderly as grand master workman, to the city to stage a rally. Four thousand people—an astonishing number in a population of about seventeen thousand, five hundred—attended. While Sovereign's visit drew few new recruits (probably because of the Knights' well-known romanticism), the crowd was an indication of Portland workers' openness to labor's agenda.

The issues that concerned Portland's laboring classes in general were of particular moment to the city's carpenters, of whom there were, by

informal count, approximately three hundred. For, as the decade of the
1880s began, carpenters in Portland faced the problems McGuire had identified nationwide as their greatest obstacles to steady work and a decent
standard of living.

Wooden columns, gingerbread, and ornamentation of the Victorian
house handmade by craftsmen, were being replaced by mass-produced
items increasingly used by architects and contractors. In commerce and
industry, builders had forsaken wood as a primary structural material in
favor of iron and steel. New, efficient machinery sent ever more lumber to
the jobsite in a semifinished condition, eliminating much handwork. The
lack of control over entry into the craft through a rigorous apprenticeship
system and the casual use of the term "carpenter" by anyone wishing to
hire out in a woodworking capacity adulterated the carpenters' level of
skill and prestige.

The effect of these developments was a general shrinkage of wages
and jobs for carpenters. Moreover, the westerner's traditional antipathy
toward sources of cheaper labor, whether Chinese, convict (contractors
leased gangs of prisoners at extremely low wages for many projects), wom-
en or children (also known as "green hands"), was prevalent among woodworkers.

There had been a local union of shipwrights in Portland since the
1870s, but they were neither powerful nor much interested in representing
other elements of the trade. McGuire's two-year-old union, however, was
gaining nationwide momentum because of the freedom it allowed locals in
administering their own affairs and its vigorous cadre of organizers. One
of these was a man named Whitten, who arrived in Portland in the summer
from San Francisco, where the carpenters were already established, and
began recruiting the nucleus of a new chapter.

After a few preliminary meetings, some forty of Portland's carpenters
gathered at Mechanics' Hall, on Second Street, on 22 September 1883, to
ratify the charter granted the new Portland Local No. 50 by the United
Brotherhood of Carpenters and Joiners of America.[9]

The new local began with great optimism. "We start with a strong
membership and many applications are coming into us," its corresponding
secretary informed the readers of *The Carpenter* magazine. He went on to

detail the conditions under which carpenters labored as they became unionized in Portland:

> Building has been brisk the past season but now it is quite slack owing to the rainy season coming on which will last until next June; very little work can be done in the Winter and Spring. The supply of carpenters is equal to the demand and far in excess at times. The wages vary from $3.00 to $3.50 per day and carpenters work harder and faster than anyplace I was ever in. Cost of living is high.[10]

Local No. 50 financed its operations and activities through an initiation fee of two dollars and a monthly dues charge of fifty cents from each member. A fine of twenty-five cents was levied if a member failed to attend one meeting per month. The union paid ten dollars per week in accident benefits up to a maximum of fifty dollars. The local also declared at its inception that, as of 1 May 1884, its members would consider nine hours a full day's work (they then worked ten), with the hours running 7:00 A.M. to 12:00 noon and 1:00 to 5:00 P.M.[11] "Union men will not work with non-union men who refuse to comply," the corresponding secretary stated flatly.[12]

As the fall wore on, Local No. 50 gathered strength. "Our union is prospering beyond our most sanguine expectations," the secretary wrote.[13] He noted an increase in membership to seventy, indicating an initiation rate of forty per month, and forecasted two hundred members by the winter. Optimism was so strong that a committee had been formed to find a larger meeting hall. The secretary wrote of holding a "grand ball" soon [14] and boasted that Local 50's members were "first-class mechanics" (the highest accolade one craftsman could bestow upon another was "mechanic"), all of whom were employed while others remained idle as work grew increasingly scarce.[15]

The permanent officers elected for the first six months of 1884 were D.C. McDonald, president; J.L. Johnson, vice president; E.T. Carr, recording secretary; William Krider, corresponding secretary; G.R. Hewitt, financial secretary; James Doherty, treasurer; John Bell, conductor; and B.H. Barcklay, warden. In February that year, Krider noted in his report in

The Carpenter, there was less cause for optimism and enthusiasm. Attendance at the weekly meetings had declined, he wrote, and "a great many of the union boys (more than half the membership, in fact) are out of work. This winter is the hardest for carpenters for several years; there is scarcely any building . . . and what little there is, one cannot work outside on account of so much rain."[16]

The spring was grimmer yet. "Mechanics and laborers are advised to stay away from Portland, Oregon, as the number of unemployed there is appalling," the secretary wrote bluntly in April.[17] A primary reason for the unemployment was an economic decline occasioned by weakness in the price of Northern Pacific stock. With the completion of the rail line, which caused large numbers of unemployed gandy dancers and other rail-gang workers to drift into Portland looking for work, as well as the convict leasing system, the stagnation in the economy posed a threat to the union. Members of No. 50 received wages of from $3.50 to $4.00 per day, but contractors were able to hire eager men for from $2.00 to $3.00 a day when they had jobs to fill.[18]

The unemployment was so bad at the outset of summer that one of the local's principal goals had to be abandoned temporarily. Krider explained that Local No. 50 had decided to postpone the strike for nine hours (planned since the union's formation), as the influx of immigrant carpenters, the lack of jobs, and low wages made such an action impractical. Moreover, he wrote, "our union is at a standstill at present."[19]

Hard times did not dampen the secretary's optimism. He emphasized that the nine-hour movement awaited only a more favorable economic climate and that the local planned to act when it arrived. Meanwhile, the membership turned to pressing matters of internal discipline. A member named James Pride was expelled for taking piecework, indicating at once the seriousness with which carpenters viewed such an act and the straitened conditions of Portland's construction industry. Another member found himself under investigation for allegedly taking a subcontract and hiring cheaper, nonunion carpenters to execute it.[20] The secretary commented, "The Union is determined to make an example of such members preferring to have a few good men than a crowd that do not pay any attention to their obligations."[21]

Even though stalled on its nine-hour initiative, weakened by hard times and a shrinking membership, and demoralized by lapses from the labor faith, Local No. 50 persevered through the summer with expanding its agenda and the arena of its activities. It joined a central organization called the Amalgamated Trade and Labor Union of Oregon, an early congress of labor organizations. Krider estimated that the unions could muster a bloc of six hundred to eight hundred votes for pro-labor candidates for the state legislature.[22] The carpenters specifically wished to elect men who would advocate the abolition of convict labor and the adoption of a mechanic's lien law. Legally, a carpenter or other workman had no recourse on defaulted bills and could not seize the property of a debtor in lieu of cash. In the fluid semifrontier society of Portland in 1884, where strangers came and went with regularity, this was a real problem for independent craftsmen.[23]

As things developed, September 1883 proved to have been an inopportune time to organize the local, for the stagnation that dampened business later that autumn and in the winter of 1884 became a recession that lasted through 1885. Local No. 50's reports to *The Carpenter* became sporadic and gloomy, interspersed occasionally with the odd note of optimism. "Trade is duller here than it has been for three or four years and a good many of our members have left the city," read the note for July 1884. Worse, wages had fallen fifty cents per day. Nevertheless, the local was "alive and awake," with new members still enrolling.[24]

"Business is still very dull here, but Spring is at hand and we hope for better times," said the local's note of April 1885.[25] But the optimism was apparently unfounded: Local No. 50 disappeared from *The Carpenter*'s pages (it submitted no notes for "Trade Section Reports," its secretaries were not listed, and it filed no financial statements) until March 1887. Then, in August that year, the Seventh Annual Report of the General Secretary of the United Brotherhood of Carpenters listed it as a reorganized union. The nine-hour demand seems to have been fulfilled in that time, because business is listed as "very dull" with wages at "$2.50-$3.00 for nine hours."[26] The wages represent a precipitous decline from those at the union's birth.

The revival of Local No. 50, probably largely predicated on the resurgence of Portland's economy, may have been tied in some measure to the resuscitation of the Federated Trades Assembly in the same year. The assembly's own reemergence can be traced to the return to Portland of Samuel Gompers, representing a much-enhanced AFL.[27] Both the AFL and the Carpenters' Union had been tested and toughened by events that had occurred since their inception, and it is possible that Gompers's newfound prestige rekindled labor activism among Portland's unionists, including the carpenters.

Gompers revived the moribund Federated Trades Assembly by restructuring the organization to eliminate some of its old problems. Under the new plan, each union was to have equal representation and was to be charged a flat yearly tax.[28] When he left the city, the assembly consisted of fifteen unions representing some four hundred men, figures that testify equally to the severity of the recession of 1883, the intrinsic faults of the original assembly, and Gompers's organizational skills.

However, the struggles of Local No. 50 were not over. Economic well-being brought its own miseries. Portland and the rest of Oregon were still regarded as "the frontier" in the late 1880s (as, indeed, they were) and still attracted large numbers of immigrants from the East and Middle West seeking their fortunes. Hence the frustration in the corresponding secretary's description of Local No. 50's activities in May 1889:

> There is an abundance of work but it is advertised so largely in the eastern states by speculators that myriad strangers are coming in daily, and are flooding the town. Many men are unemployed. Since May 1st we are rigidly enforcing the card system and all the building trades are standing by each other in refusing to work with non-union men.[29]

The "working card" system was the one method by which the fledgling unions could enforce their agreements with employers and ensure a wholly union crew. The system was based on the issuance of a card denoting paid-up membership in the union. Enforcement was undertaken by so-called "walking delegates," forerunners of the modern business agent. The walking delegates were part-time, usually unpaid, unionists, whose charge was to travel from worksite to worksite observing conditions on the job and checking cards.[30] The steady stream of new workers arriving in Portland almost constantly, and the volunteer status of the walking delegates, made the card system almost impossible to implement thoroughly or to police effectively. With three thousand unionists in Portland by 1889, not all of whom were always current in their dues payments, the wonder is not that it failed after a sporadic existence of a year or so, but that it was attempted at all.

In retrospect, the economic inconsistencies of the mid-1880s were not enough to destroy the impulse of Portland's carpenters and other laborers to combine in unions. Although the growth of the carpenters' union was severely retarded by the difficulties, by the end of the decade woodworkers had reemerged to the forefront of Portland's labor movement and by 1890 were caught up in a significant struggle between the forces of labor and management.

TWO
"Eight Hours Will Constitute a Day's Work . . ."

EARLY IN THE HISTORY OF THE LABOR movement, most of the rank-and-file members of the carpenters' and other craft unions, in common with Samuel Gompers and Peter McGuire, regarded strikes with profound distaste. Typically, where political action was concerned, craft unionists held views similar to those of independent artisans or small shopkeepers. They were reluctant to submerge their identities and freedom of action in mass movements, still less to impel those movements toward their goals through violence of the kind that strikes seemed inevitably to engender, or to any other action that might seem to hold the American economic system to ransom.

Gompers and McGuire were proponents of what came to be called "business unionism." They saw the movement as being no different from employers' organizations. "The trade unions are the business organizations of the wage earners," Gompers said. Neither they nor the unionists of the AFL were revolutionaries. They were not hostile to capitalism, although Gompers had once been a Marxist and McGuire remained a socialist. They sought merely to improve wages and the conditions under which wages were earned. Above all, the AFL leaders wished to make a place for the labor movement as a legitimate and dignified American institution. The strike, at least to the late-nineteenth-century mind, led only to radicalism and anarchy.

Yet from 1877 onward, there was a steady increase in strikes, lockouts, and other conflicts throughout the nation in every significant industry. In 1886, a pivotal year for labor, approximately six hundred ten thousand Americans were idled by strikes, lockouts, or shutdowns arising from strikes. This figure represented a 30 percent increase over the average of the five previous years.[1]

Under the circumstances, labor leaders came quickly to understand that they must put themselves at the head of their followers' growing militance if they wanted to retain control of the movement. By the same token, employers had responded to labor activism with tough, often ruthless, tactics. Jay Gould put it bluntly when he said, "I can hire one-half the working class to kill the other half." After the savagery of the Haymarket riot, the average strike seemed sedate. Men like Gompers and McGuire were thus forced to include the strike in their arsenal of weapons.

One issue on which even the most conservative union men agreed was worth striking for was the eight-hour day. As early as 1866, labor leaders dreamed of reducing the hours of work while maintaining the same rate of pay. William Sylvis endorsed the eight-hour day and so even did Terence Powderly, although he had reservations about whether the "horny fisted sons of toil," as he called the members of the Knights of Labor, should strike for it. In 1869, the federal government gave some legitimacy to the movement when President Ulysses S. Grant issued an executive order bestowing the eight-hour day on government workers. After the financial crash of 1873, however, the order was rescinded. Eight-hour leagues sprang up in large cities across the United States. The leagues' anthem had a verse that summed up their ideal and intent: "Eight hours for work, eight hours for rest/Eight hours for what we will!"

McGuire, in particular, recognized the benefits of the shortened workday for unions and their rank and file. Shorter work hours could only strengthen the United Brotherhood of Carpenters by creating more jobs; more jobs meant more potential recruits for the union. The individual would gain more leisure, and more leisure might lead to self-improvement.[2] In late-nineteenth-century America, self-improvement was almost as powerful a cult as it is today. The myth of the self-made man, epitomized by Abraham Lincoln, and what needed to be done to become one, drove people to buy books like Samuel Smiles's *Self Help* and the Horatio Alger stories, with their inspirational tales of rags-to-riches success.[3]

Although the eight-hour day had been attained by some carpenters' locals, including Brooklyn's and Baltimore's, in the aftermath of the Civil War the shorter day had been lost quickly, a casualty of the same economic disaster that had ended the federal government's eight-hour experiment. However, the goal remained on the union's agenda. By 1886, the United Brotherhood of Carpenters had taken the lead among labor organizations in pursuing it, both because it was a moral question for McGuire and because it was an issue that attracted new members to the union.[4]

McGuire started with an intermediate goal—the nine-hour day. In 1883, Local No. 50 and all other Pacific Coast locals in the building trades had won it (though for Local No. 50, it was short-lived)—the best regional performance in the carpenters' network. But in the wake of the bloodshed at Haymarket Square, where the lead demonstration in the national effort on behalf of the eight-hour day took place, the entire labor movement and its agenda fell into disrepute. Organized labor could only regroup, gather its strength, and wait for the propitious moment to launch another assault on the citadel of long hours.

By 1889, that moment seemed to have arrived. The AFL had been reorganized and revitalized by Gompers and McGuire, and as the decade drew to a close, the United Brotherhood of Carpenters had emerged as the strongest of the AFL affiliates. The Knights of Labor, and Powderly, the reluctant dragon of the labor movement, had begun their long slide into oblivion, thus offering less resistance to unified mass action and less confusion in defining and pursuing labor's objectives.

Because of their prestige among the crafts, the vigor of their organization, and the charisma of their leader, the carpenters were selected by

Gompers to lead the renewed effort for the eight-hour day, beginning on 1 May 1890 with a national strike. In Portland, planning for the strike had begun in 1888. As in other cities, the carpenters of Local No. 50 were to assume leadership of the campaign, with the rest of the building trades unions to go out with them.

Portland's labor community was encouraged about the possibilities for success in the new round of agitation. The union card system seemed to promise control of the labor supply to the unions and, therefore, a dramatic and complete shutdown of construction if demands were not met. The building trades also had their own walking delegate who could coordinate, inform, and rally the building trades. Furthermore, the viability of the Federated Trades Assembly appeared to promote uniform support among all the member unions of the city. Captain John O'Brien, a typesetter and a somewhat enigmatic figure who headed the assembly, urged the Portland unions unaffiliated with their national headquarters to make the necessary connections in anticipation of the parent organizations' support. A rally at the Masonic Hall on Labor Day, 2 September 1889, caused further optimism as allies of labor, including Oregon's colorful, if erratic, governor, Sylvester Pennoyer, spoke in favor of the cause.

Among the reasons Portland's unions wanted the eight-hour day, the most significant was that there were still not enough jobs in the city to go around.[5] The flow of immigrants had continued throughout the decade. Among the many resolutions adopted at the Labor Day rally was one that addressed the problem. It demanded a prohibition on "the employment of other than citizens of the state," the enforcement of laws, and the bringing of criminals to justice.[6]

The apparent solidarity of the labor community was, however, not without fissures. For one thing, the construction trades unions, under the leadership of Local No. 50, had formed Portland's first trade sectional, the Building Trades League, in the summer of 1889.[7] The carpenters had urged its formation when they were unable to get approval from the Federated Trades Assembly to assign a walking delegate solely to the construction industry. The Building Trades League then hired its own delegate. As the largest and most prestigious union in the city, the carpenters were the object of natural jealousy and suspicion from other unions, but the rapid formation of the Building Trades League caused some smaller unions to charge that the carpenters were trying to undermine the Federated Trades Assembly simply for thwarting their will.[8] The Building Trades League's walking delegate thus became a symbol of division as well as unity.

Another problem was that the level of commitment among the building trades to the principle of eight hours was not uniform. The carpenters constituted the only union openly dedicated to a strike for the shorter day and its corollaries, such as no wage reduction. On 5 December 1889, the carpenters had announced for the eight-hour day, though they said nothing about wages. The notice was also laconic about a strike and even promised to finish buildings under construction should there be one.[9] A note in *The Carpenter* dated 15 March 1890 said of the situation in Portland, "Carpenters, painters, plumbers, and trimmers have all notified their employers that after May 1, 1890, eight hours will constitute a day's work."[10] While this indicated a level of solidarity hitherto lacking, the fact remained that Local No. 50 was to bear the major responsibility for the movement.

By the end of the winter, only the uninformed among Portland's citizens could have been ignorant of what was coming. The eight-hour-day movement had assumed the proportions of a tidal wave—a classic case of an idea whose time had come, if newspapers across the country were to be believed—not only in Portland and the rest of America, but in all of Europe, including England. The carpenters would not be denied the shorter working day, whether a strike were necessary or not, no matter how unevenly other unions marched on its behalf.

The carpenters' well-understood intent created yet more difficulties for labor before the strike. The Builders' Exchange, the Portland contractors' trade organization, which was acknowledged by labor to be as well prepared for the struggle as labor itself, began a campaign to preempt public sympathy for the would-be strikers and even to stigmatize them. O'Brien complained to the *Oregonian*, for instance, that some important construction projects, such as one on Holton House, had been characterized by the builders as being stalled because of the restiveness of labor, when, in reality, the builder was merely awaiting the preparation of the lot.[11] Similarly, William S. Ladd, a well-known financier and developer, was said to be reluctant to go ahead with a large project when, according to O'Brien, he had been unable to obtain the property on which he wanted to build.[12]

As the date for the strike neared, labor-management relations grew tense. Suspicions and resentment smoldered in both camps. With charges and countercharges flying in the press, all that was needed for a major confrontation was a small gesture or incident from either side. On 16 April, some of the members of Local No. 50 walked off a job in an effort to get a nonunion man fired. The Builders' Exchange, which had maintained discipline among contractors by fining members $150 for dismissing nonunion workers, retaliated by locking out all union carpenters. This was undoubtedly a shock to the carpenters, who on 24 February had walked off another project, taking all the other trades with them, over the presence of a scab carpenter. Within ninety minutes the man had been fired and work resumed.[13]

In the face of all the careful planning and preparation nationwide for the eight-hour-day movement, Portland's carpenters now had a premature strike on their hands. Unfortunately, the central issue had all but faded from sight as they made additional demands, of which the most important were the closed shop, unlimited access for the walking delegate to construction sites, and immediate unionization of immigrant mechanics. These were so repugnant to the contractors that they stiffened their resistance. The confrontation became a struggle for power and the legitimacy of labor unions.

The Builders' Exchange made this clear when, on 30 April, they placed a rambling, somewhat perfervid broadside in the *Oregonian* that nevertheless put the contractors firmly on the attack in the dispute. Their "Declaration of Principles of Non-Union Mechanics" read in part:

> WHEREAS certain societies known as "unions" and associated under the name of the "Union Building Trades League," have made known ... purposes which if consummated, will destroy individual liberty not alone for the workingman, but for all citizens who contemplate, or who have begun the erection of any buildings thereby subjecting the whole community to a tyranny too galling to be endured and too humiliating to be tolerated for an hour: Therefore be it

RESOLVED: That we will use every lawful means within our power to prevent this usurpation of the rights of the individual, this effort at centralization of power in the hands of any body of men. . . . That we denounce as rank injustice the demand that union men will be given preference under all circumstances. . . .

That [the principle that only those workers who can show a union card can work] . . . by exhibiting the certificate of slavery to the "walking delegate" is one that only needs to be stated to be appreciated by a long suffering public.

That we recommend as a proper solution of existing troubles absolute industrial freedom;

That we have unbounded confidence that the American people will settle the question by deciding that communism, the spectre which directs this attack on the liberties of the people, shall not be the law of the land.[14]

The early opening of hostilities threw the carpenters and the Federated Trades Assembly a little off stride. The initiative and the moral advantage had clearly been lost, at least temporarily. Only on 1 May did the bricklayers, plasterers, and laborers walk out in sympathy with Local No. 50. Meanwhile, the assembly passed a resolution modifying its original plan for financial support of the strikers. On 3 April, the Federated Trades Assembly had decided to assess each union member 10 percent of his week's wages for the eight-hour movement. All unions that participated in the strike were to keep the funds they collected. The funds of any union not on strike were to be diverted to the carpenters.[15] However, as a long war of attrition loomed, the assembly prepared to increase the strike fund. Yet it took until 30 April to get a vote to expand the assessment on individual unionists' one day's pay each week.[16]

Labor's disarray, catalyzed by the premature walkout of the carpenters, was modified a little on 1 May. The nationwide demonstrations for eight hours that day, involving 550 locals in 452 cities, once again focused debate on the real issue and legitimized the strike in Portland. The *Oregonian*, generally a conservative, establishment organ, endorsed the strike,

calling the eight-hour movement international in scope and "long defer-
red."[17]

In what may have been a sign of weakness disguised by the rhetoric of
toughness, the Builders' Exchange appealed to the strikers to return to
work, threatening to replace sympathy strikers with nonunion workers if
plasterers, stonemasons and bricklayers did not return on prelockout
terms. No concessions—specifically not that of the eight-hour day—were
offered.[18]

This belligerence was belied by the announcement on the same day
that some contractors sympathetic to the eight-hour movement had with-
drawn from the Builders' Exchange and formed an organization known as
the Master Builders' Association, with the intention of reorganizing the
unions. Desperate, the Builders' Exchange demanded that mills sell lumber only to its members. Governor Sylvester Pennoyer, the owner of a
sawmill, refused to cooperate, again lending badly needed prestige to the
strikers' cause.[19]

For the carpenters, the strike was having one desirable effect. It was
attracting new members to the union, which boasted that it had grown to
eight hundred and thirty members, two hundred of whom worked for
members of the Master Builders' Association.[20] On the other hand, as the
Oregonian reported, Portlanders were becoming tired of the strike, which,
moreover, was crippling the city's economy. The newspaper estimated
that by 11 May the strikers had lost $150,000 in wages, and the contractors
much more in profits. Meanwhile, Portland had stopped growing.[21]

Anxiety to resolve the dispute began to emerge. It was bruited about
that the Builders' Exchange had been prepared to grant the eight-hour day
with no reduction in daily pay. The president of the Exchange, Joseph C.
Bayer, eventually confirmed the rumor, saying that it was the additional
demands, which seemed to restrict employers' freedom of action, that had
stiffened their backs.[22]

The resolve of the unions, so severely tested in the unanticipated
beginning of the strike, was starting to weaken. The carpenters remained
reasonably firm, but the unions striking in sympathy were less sure of their
ground. It was not surprising, therefore, that on 11 May the bricklayers,

speaking for the Union Building Trades League, proffered a greatly reduced list of demands to the contractors. The unions simply required the
eight-hour day and the nine-hour daily rate of three dollars, with time and
a half for overtime and double time for Sunday.[23] The other, more trouble-
some, demands were dropped.

The Builders' Exchange, apparently confident that victory was within
reach, played for time, waiting for the collapse of the strike effort. Bayer
reported that contractors were deeply concerned about an eight-hour
working day in Oregon's climate, where the building season could last for
only six months. Moreover, he said, the eight-hour movement might become an epidemic, spreading to other unions in every field. The increased
cost of production resulting from the eight-hour day would pervade the
nation's economy. The workingman would suffer most as the cost of living
rose accordingly.

In fact, both the builders and the Building Trades League had mis-
judged the situation. The carpenters—the key to any settlement—rejected
both the proposal of the bricklayers and the posturing of Bayer. They
stayed out even as the sympathy strikers, still supportive of them, went
back to work in mid-May.

The *Oregonian*, reflecting the mixed view many Portlanders probably
held of the situation, editorialized that, as labor had made so many concessions, the employers should grant the eight-hour day.[24] The editor added,
however, that workingmen should aspire to a higher station in life. To
achieve a better status required that a man earn more than was possible in a
mere eight hours. Ten was more like it. He concluded that the eight-hour
day was not a good thing.

The contractors' insistence that the bricklayers' compromise be put in
writing only produced further stalling and subsequent rejection. Fortu-
nately for the carpenters, this, together with the *Oregonian*'s sympathetic
or at least neutral reporting, was what engaged the public's attention,
rather than the union's own recalcitrance. Its mounting losses and the split
in its ranks, coupled with the heralded mortality of the eight-hour issue
and the expression of the public attitude in labor's favor, finally put the
builders again on the defensive. The pressure to resolve their differences
with labor settled on them. A massive rally of workingmen on 20 May in

downtown Portland proved that, though the carpenters' was the only union still striking, labor continued to support them wholeheartedly.

With the handwriting so clearly on the wall, Bayer came to the bargaining table the next day. In an anticlimactic settlement, the Builders' Exchange gave up the eight-hour day. The carpenters conceded the pay issue, agreeing to accept the same hourly rate as under nine hours. (Thus they would have fared better under the bricklayers' proposal.)

A subsidiary effect of the strike was that it discredited the Builders' Exchange, which collapsed as the Master Builders' Association survived. A more liberal organization, the Multnomah Builders' Exchange, came into being. The new organization was not affiliated with the National Builders' Exchange, a highly conservative group that unfailingly opposed labor and fostered the same attitude in its branches.

The strike also enhanced the eminence of Local No. 50 in union circles, increased its standing among potential recruits, and augmented the image of vigor and dedication to the rights of workers all unionists wished to foster among the general public. Most significantly, the carpenters introduced to Portland an idea of great simplicity that had immense ramifications for the economic and social structure of the city: the belief that a worker should labor for only eight hours a day.

THREE
Era of Confrontation

IN 1893, THE TWENTY-YEAR CYCLE OF BOOM
and bust that had regularly afflicted the American economy since the panic of 1819 once again plunged down-
ward. Despite various warning recessions, such as that of 1884, the people
and the government were unprepared for the collapse, and all classes suffered reverses. The workers were hurt worst of all and, disregarding the
obvious distress of their employers, tended to blame them for their miseries. This attitude was not without foundation, as the business wing of
the Republican party and the conservative Democratic administration of
Grover Cleveland, dominant through the 1880s and into the 1890s, were
largely responsible for the problem.

Portland did not escape the effects of the depression. Probably as
much as half the labor force was unemployed during its worst period.[1] A
number of financial institutions and other businesses, as well as their principals, among whom were some of the city's leading lights, were adversely
affected, either temporarily or permanently.[2]

Nationally, railroads, banks, and factories failed. Embittered workers struck plants and marched on Washington, D.C., descending on the capital like locusts.[3] Class differences widened as mutual suspicion deepened, and a chasm of hostility opened between management and labor that would take decades to heal.

In Portland, with both the Union Pacific and the Northern Pacific in bankruptcy, economic activity halted. The construction industry was crippled as housing, street, and rail construction stopped. Lumber mills swallowed huge inventories of unsalable wood products. One contemporary observer later recalled seeing the unemployed in tattered clothing, without shoes, and hungry.[4]

Yet for organized labor the 1890s were not particularly difficult. The depression, to be sure, left an almost insuperable distrust of the city's business elite in the minds of workingmen after its brief, intense run—a distrust that would haunt both sides in the next century. However, the overwhelming impression was of a frontier economy in a growing city bursting with energy, optimism, and plans for a prosperous future.

While the rank and file felt the depression's sting, the unions benefited from the city's rapid growth. The Federated Trades Assembly, crippled by a chronic lack of funds except in times of crisis, was dominated by its strongest unions—those in the building trades, most particularly Local No. 50. Affiliated with the most prestigious union in the nation and the heroes of the eight-hour day, the carpenters attracted a steady stream of new members and generally kept them working.

The assembly was briefly challenged at the time by an organization known as the Central Labor Council. However, the council was a creature of the Knights of Labor, which was itself in decline.[5] Thanks largely to the power of the Carpenters' Union and its links to the AFL, the Federated Trades Assembly was able to withstand the Central Labor Council's challenge to its role as Portland's Labor Central.[6] But it was on shaky ground thereafter, and by 1889 it was reorganized as the Federated Trades Council. In its turn, the Federated Trades Council later became the Central Labor Council, although that group had no connection with the previous organization of the same name.

By 1902, three delegates from No. 50—Christian Bomberger, C.W. Ryan, and William F. Caldwell—represented the carpenters' interests and played a significant role in the Federated Trades Council. Three delegates from No. 50 continued to sit on the Building Trades Council. These men, and the union they represented, had a disproportionate influence on Portland's labor affairs for three main reasons:

UNION CARPENTERS were highly regarded for their proficiency by local contractors and, in light of Portland's building boom, were constantly employed. This was reflected in the attraction Portland held for carpenters from elsewhere, who migrated with vexing regularity, threatening the jobs of the residents while keeping the union growing. By 1902, between ten and twelve carpenters were joining the union at every meeting.[7]

CONTRACTORS generally accepted and respected the goals of business unionism and its leaders. A corollary to this was that the craft was still the most skilled in the labor movement, which gave it continued status among the other trades.

THE UNITED BROTHERHOOD of Carpenters' national record was one of vigor and success—prima facie evidence, as it were, of its effectiveness. Out of 150 strike movements throughout the United States in the first six months of 1902, the brotherhood succeeded in every instance.[8]

An example of Local No. 50's position in the city's economic affairs was evident in the autumn of 1902, when nearly one thousand carpenters signed a statement condemning a plan to build a drydock in Vancouver, Washington. The drydock's site was soon changed to Portland.[9]

Also in 1902, the carpenters tried to extend their influence to the level of state politics by nominating Bomberger for state labor commissioner. A general vote by members of the Federated Trades Council of Oregon, however, resulted in support for another unionist.

Local No. 50 was not merely parochial in its concerns. From a treasury swelled by the recent surge in membership, the union sent fifteen hundred dollars of its general-fund monies to support striking coal miners in Pennsylvania and West Virginia in October 1902. For a local union at the time, it was a princely sum.[10]

The strike in the East's anthracite coal fields, as well as one in Belgium that threatened to turn into a revolution, arrested the attention of the world that year. These events, together with a strike of textile workers at Oregon City, a mill-by-mill strike of the newly organized lumber mill workers of Portland, and the pay increase won by the new laundry workers' union of Portland, constituted the backdrop for the formation of yet another labor organization in which Local No. 50 played a significant role.

On 5, 6, and 7 May in Portland, in an atmosphere charged with worldwide labor unrest, the first convention of the Oregon State Federation of Labor was held. One observer remarked that the gathering seemed like a religious revival.[11]

The convention was brought about by George Y. Harry, delegate to the Federated Trades Council from the Sheet Metal Workers. After badgering the council to sponsor a statewide labor organization for months, in March he had been authorized by the Federated Trades Council to make a thirty-day tour of Oregon, to create interest in a convention of all the state's unions. His success was indicated by the fact that the new unions he instituted in the smaller cities and towns as he traveled still lacked charters by their national offices when their delegates arrived in Portland.[12]

The nine delegates from Local No. 50 were Thomas P. French, William H. Brackett, Elmer Melton, Frank Manion, C.W. Ryan, John I. Murray, Park McDonald, S.E. Lorrall, and Samuel McKee.

The convention is of interest for the obvious reason that it marked the beginning of Oregon's most influential labor organization. To remark on Local No. 50's role in its origin is, of course, also important. It is, however, most illuminating to note the resolutions that the convention passed. We may, with some confidence, regard them as expressions of the mind and will of the state's labor community with respect to social, economic, and political improvement for the working class. More to the point, in view of the position of leadership of the carpenters of Local No. 50 within the labor movement, it is likely that the resolutions expressed their mind and will as they entered the twentieth century.

Far from being the prescription for radicalism that the times might seem to have demanded, the resolutions voted out by the Oregon State

Federation of Labor were a model of the mainstream progressivism then current up and down the West Coast.[13] Zealously but rationally reformist, they called for changes that would benefit most of society, while defending labor's special interests.

The convention demanded the direct election of senators. It supported an amendment to the state constitution providing for the initiative and referendum, the direct primary for nominating candidates for public office, and an agency for the regulation of public utilities. It also called for the expropriation of private utilities.[14] All this was the standard progressive medicine for what ailed the political process, but, in the event of acceptance, meant that labor, voting and acting as a bloc, would have more power and leverage in Oregon politics than previously. Private utilities flew in the face of three decades of agitation at every level of government and the popular wisdom on the subject of monopolies.

The delegates also called for the creation of a state bureau of labor and the abolition of convict and child labor, as well as the exclusion of Japanese and Chinese workers. They denounced the use of the injunction as an antistrike weapon. Cheap labor of any kind distorted wage scales and took jobs from trade union members, who were exclusively white males. Child labor was distasteful to industrial unions in which assembly-line workers did not need to be especially strong or skilled. Convicts were the nemesis of the building trades in particular, as contractors were able to hire gangs of them at a stunningly low figure to do road building and maintenance.

Asians were another, more complex, matter. As we have seen, the early labor movement of Portland coalesced in part around anti-Chinese sentiment.[15] All over the West Coast, the Chinese, and the Japanese (who were later in arriving), were objects of the suspicion, ignorance, prejudice, and violence of all classes of whites. The Asians' willingness to accept much lower wages and poorer working conditions than Caucasian workers in general, and trade unionists in particular, in itself guaranteed the enmity of the labor movement. The economic argument against toleration of the immigrants, compounded by their industry, their willingness to work at anything, and their skill in doing so, was coupled with a race hatred fueled by journalists and politicians from California to Washington. This attitude energized the labor movement and made "imported labor"—as it was sometimes euphemistically called—the special bane of West Coast unionists.[16]

Finally, by the end of the nineteenth century, the use of the judicial injunction by employers as a weapon to break strikes approached the status of an art form. The Sherman Anti-Trust Act of 1890, for example, was used against labor, whereas its framers had intended it for use against capital. To unionists, it frequently seemed that the courts and the monied interests were in league against them, stopping their offensives against economic and social injustice with a mere slip of paper provided by some black-robed judge with no social conscience. They were not always wrong.

In October 1902, President Theodore Roosevelt reversed the trend when the anthracite mine operators petitioned him to issue an injunction to call out the army, if necessary, to get their striking miners back to work on their terms. Instead, the president gave them to understand that he might call out troops to seize the mines if the owners did not abandon their "arrogant stupidity" and submit to arbitration. They complied.

In light of its activism, its proliferating organizations and the length of its agenda, it would be logical to conclude that Portland's labor movement was secure and successful. However, the success of the business unions was superficial. So far as the goals of ambitious organizations such as the carpenters were concerned, more remained undone than had been accomplished. Their previous triumphs gave them an illusion of power, while their adversaries became more wary of their intentions than was warranted by their record. This meant that fundamentally conservative unions like Local No. 50 were in a paradoxical position. If they wished to redeem the promise of the labor movement and the vision of men like McGuire (who by the turn of the century had passed from the scene), they must continually press forward in the fight for higher wages, better hours, and improved conditions. Yet they must also preserve what they had already won and not antagonize employers too greatly. Thus the carpenters developed a cautious, middle-class brand of reformism and labor activism that made labor radicals impatient and sometimes confused employers.

This led to a period of instability and confrontation in Portland's labor-management relations, characterized by vacillation on the part of the Carpenters' Union between the two poles of its personality and over-reaction to it by their employers.

Shortly after the convention, the carpenters became embroiled in a labor dispute on behalf of another union that was to have repercussions for Local No. 50. In May, the Building Trades Council told Portland contractors that all twelve of its affiliated unions would go out on a general strike if planing mills did not grant a nine-hour day to members of the Amalgamated Woodworkers Union. J.E. Lawton, Local No. 50's delegate to the council and its secretary, said that the carpenters particularly championed the woodworkers because of their own struggle to gain shorter hours. By 21 May, 95 percent of the city's union carpenters had walked off their jobs in support of the woodworkers. Work on the Failing Building, which was to become a Portland landmark for many years, the Weinhard Building, and the headquarters of the Lawrence Leather Company and Findlay's undertaking business was halted as a result.

Officials of No. 50 remained in the forefront of the dispute. Lawton charged that the planing-mill operators' claim that shorter hours for their employees would prevent them from competing with sawmills was specious, as the planing mills turned out finer work than the sawmills. Thus there was no basis for comparison.[17] Bomberger, meanwhile, joined the *Oregon Journal* in a call for arbitration. A mill owner, however, responded flatly, "We have nothing to arbitrate."[18] The operators' recalcitrance derived from the fact that the lumber market was slack. This allowed them to work with green hands at reduced capacity without much fear of losing profits, produced a split in the ranks of labor, and prematurely ended the building trades' participation in the strike.

The carpenters, despite the public recognition of their delegates and the solid front they presented in leaving their work, had gone out only reluctantly. They had not approved of the general strike, preferring a boycott of unfair building materials.[19] When a Federated Trades Council arbitration committee approached the Building Trades Council about this concept, the carpenters backed it. The rest of the Building Trades Council sided with them, leaving the Woodworkers' Union (which was not a member of the Building Trades Council) to picket alone.

The painters' union, a more militant group, was incensed. Its spokes-man accused the Federated Trades Assembly of fomenting the strike, then abandoning it. The *Labor Press*, on the other hand, endorsed the carpen-ters' point of view, which, in sum, was that the strike was hurting innocent and friendly businessmen.[20] The newspaper called the carpenters and their allies on the issue "older and more conservative men."[21]

Whether or not it had hurt them, contractors and other businessmen were outraged by the general strike. Some contractors stated flatly that the unions would have to work with whatever building materials were on hand, fair or unfair. Sawmill owners and materials dealers became in-volved when they announced their intention not to provide building ma-terials to contractors observing the Building Trades Council boycott.

The unions were weakened by business's united front. Short of a prolonged, arduous, and general strike, there seemed no alternative but to comply with the dictum of master builder contractors, who were signatory to Building Trades Council agreements. On the other hand, there was a period of "phony war," until late June, because one of the largest union sawmills kept a supply of fair lumber flowing to union construction sites. The *Oregonian* reported that its owner was running for office in a forth-coming election and needed union support.[22]

The carpenters evaded greater involvement in the strike by not ques-tioning the provenance of the lumber on a jobsite. However, if a Building Trades Council walking delegate clearly labeled materials as being unfair, the carpenters honored the boycott. By late June they were openly claim-ing that it was unjust and that because it related only to wooden materials, its effects fell disproportionately on carpenters.

On 3 July, the *Labor Press* reported that the Building Trades Council had conceded the issue and ended the boycott. A bitter coda to the episode was furnished by a spokesman for the woodworkers, who were left to carry on their battle alone. "The carpenters' union have shifted the burden of the contest," he said, "and the building Trades Council felt reluctant in passing it up to other unions who are less able to stand the brunt."[23]

Like a time bomb, the animosities between the building trades and their employers ticked away for the remainder of 1902. They exploded into full-scale labor-management warfare in February 1903, when the carpen-ters and painters announced that after 1 April they would demand a higher wage for those craftsmen not earning $3.50 per day, the standard West Coast rate.

The Master Builders' Association offered no immediate response to this declaration. While a strike over the issue seemed unlikely, the *Labor Press* nevertheless felt called upon to advise caution and fairness in any future negotiations on the matter. The paper also warned against unnamed "officious persons" who were harming organized labor by their (presumably needlessly belligerent) conduct toward businessmen.[24]

The carpenters of Local No. 50, who had largely been kept employed over the winter with as many as twelve buildings under construction, entered negotiations convinced of the justice of their cause and the aptness of their strategy to produce the desired raise while limiting damage to their relations with the contractors. They planned for those men at the lower rate to strike. In the walkout, one hundred men left their work and most found new jobs on the same day for $3.50.[25] One contractor refused his $3.00 men the higher wage and they left the site, only to be sent back by the union as their own replacements. They received $3.50.[26]

The *Oregonian* observed with studied nonchalance that this activity represented only the usual turnover in the construction industry.[27] Negotiations between the two sides were undertaken, but the charade of business as usual only precluded any frank discussion of the real issue at the heart of the disagreement.

The union saw itself as championing a uniform minimum wage, while the contractors believed they were merely defending their right to pay wages based on individual worth. But the central problem was about unskilled or underskilled craftsmen. Immigration was still bringing to the city men calling themselves carpenters who were sometimes not particularly well trained and sometimes not skilled by any reasonable standard, in addition to true journeymen carpenters.[28]

The union was well aware that its ranks included less competent workmen. In a moment of candor at the height of the strike, Bomberger told an *Oregonian* reporter:

> I know that some members of the union are nearer the laborers' class than that of carpenters, but we took them into the union simply

because they were employed as carpenters. If they were not worth carpenters' wages, they should never have been taken on as carpenters. . . . Such men were taken into the union to protect ourselves. . . .[29]

Even Local No. 50's business agent, Otha N. Pierce, was said to think that, even though the strike amounted to a major test of wills, the union should not push management too far over an issue like that of ill-qualified workmen. It would be tantamount to telling them whom they could hire.

With labor-management relations in the delicate balance, attitudes and feelings formed during the strife of the previous spring began to have an effect. The painters, who had always been more militant than the carpenters in their dealings with employers, regarded the strike as a test of power. They were prepared to make a stand that would break the contractors' resolve. More important, they were still resentful over the carpenters' actions in the millmen's strike. For that matter, they said the carpenters were not doing their part in the current difficulties. They therefore toughened their position by announcing that they would strike any contractor who refused to come up to the minimum wage. They also said that they would appeal to the Building Trades Council to have such a contractor put on the Building Trades' unfair list. No union man would then work for him.[30] On 6 April, after nonunion painters appeared at some jobsites, they made good on their threats.

The tactic apparently worked, as some Master Builders' Association members agitated within the organization to end the strike. The majority, however, tried to strengthen their hand by combining with the Master Painters' Association. This newly confident, larger organization guaranteed a protracted dispute by immediately demanding an end to the so-called "one-boss" rule imposed by the union. The rule permitted only one employer to work with a construction crew, thereby expanding the job pool.

Negotiations had made some progress before the escalation. In the give and take, the unions withdrew their demand for a right-to-strike clause in their contract. In return, the contractors conceded the $3.50 wage. Moreover, the carpenters, who pulled their men off construction sites

picketed by the painters on 6 April, had retained their standing throughout the negotiations. Referring to their concession on the right-to-strike
issue, the *Labor Press* observed, "The carpenters form one of the largest
and most influential unions in the building trades and their action is expected temporarily to stop the growth of the strike demand."

Old animosities, however, sealed the issue once again in late April,
when the Millmen's Association, perhaps out of vindictiveness over the
1902 dispute, but clearly in the hope of buttressing the alliance between the
Master Builders' and the Master Painters' associations, announced that
their lumber mills would sell wood only to members of the struck employers' associations and not to any employing union carpenters. Local No. 50
met this unexpected twist by using chapter funds to purchase lumber out
of state and ship it to Portland to supply cooperative contractors.

Despite the union's quick response to the millmen's challenge, it was
pressing for a way out of the impasse. E.A. Caldwell, president of Local
No. 50, called for a committee of the Building Trades Council to meet with
the contractors. His timing was right. Both sides were suffering from the
strike. The *Oregonian*, for instance, claimed on 9 May that carpenters were
returning to work with nonunion painters.[31] In fact, as the *Labor Press*
reported, a few had, but the rest were subsisting on doles from the union's
overtaxed strike fund. The contractors, meanwhile, were finding it difficult to continue projects with nonunion labor, whom some people frankly
characterized as "wood butchers."

By late May, what had begun as a skirmish had become a major deba-
cle for both sides. The Master Builders' Association, its members hurt
financially by construction delays, petitioned the mill owners to lift their
edict on lumber. When they did, both sides hurried to the bargaining
table. By mid-June, all eight hundred carpenters had returned to work,
mostly but not entirely at the same wage, $3.50 per day.

Ironically, those most damaged by the strike of 1903 were not the
principals—the carpenters, painters, and contractors—but the Building
Trades Council and some of its less powerful members. The strain of the
long action took a toll on relations among council members and between

the smaller unions and employers angered by the turmoil. The sheet-metal workers, for example, were locked out by their employers when they did not meet a demand to withdraw from the Building Trades Council. In order to regain their jobs, they were forced to comply.[32]

At the same time, a dispute broke out between the lathers and plasterers on the issue of jurisdiction over certain kinds of work. Both unions withdrew from the Building Trades Council. The Building Laborers' Union struck their employers without giving proper notice in accordance with Building Trades Council bylaws. The council promptly ordered them back to work, but the union instead simply resigned from the council.

By July, with the electricians locked in a bitter strike with their employers and only six of the original thirteen council members left, the Building Trades Council could no longer enforce the card system. This, in turn, meant that it no longer controlled jobs in the construction industry, which left it with little reason to exist.

The confrontation between Portland's construction unions and management began to come full circle as 1905 approached. In the summer of that year, a dream of the business community was realized when the city held the Lewis and Clark Exposition. Boosters of the city began planning in 1895 for an extravaganza that would introduce the nation and the rest of the world to the economic and cultural potential of Portland.

Residual resentment between labor and management, catalyzed by the fair, surfaced soon after the Building Trades strike. The civic elite had solicited the trade unions to buy blocks of exposition stock, promising in return that all construction work at the fairgrounds would be done by union members. After the Oregon State Legislature had appropriated fifty thousand dollars for the fair, however, the organizers denied that such a promise had been made.[33]

The construction trades reacted to the denial with outrage. Spurred by memories of business solidarity in the recent strike and old class antagonisms left over from the depression of '93, they lashed out at the businessmen in the Oregon State Federation of Labor convention at La Grande. There, Otha N. Pierce of Local No. 50 spearheaded the passage of a resolution calling for a referendum of the people on the use of tax monies to finance the exposition. (Oregon's referendum law had been passed in 1902.) On his return to Portland, Pierce began a petition drive for the referral.

This stance threatened to divide the union movement in Portland deeply. Union men who owned property in the city and those in service trades saw the fair as a potential windfall, and they were therefore violently opposed to the referendum. The exposition's directors, meanwhile, were recalcitrant. Furious over the referendum movement, they retaliated by advertising in eastern newspapers for nonunion bricklayers. Nevertheless, the *Labor Press* noted smugly, it was "a well known fact that not a brick [was] being laid at the Fairgrounds."[34]

Still, in early 1905, the construction unions remained aggrieved. The petition drive had failed. Carpenters working at the fair were on nine-hour shifts while those on projects elsewhere in the city worked eight hours. Portland, despite the *Labor Press*'s boast, was flooded with nonunion workers.

Led by the carpenters, the trade unions called a strike in March. In the face of such a grave threat to the imminent enrichment of themselves and their city, the exposition's directors came to the bargaining table and made some concessions to the unions, the most significant of which was the segregation of union and nonunion workmen at different buildings on the fairgrounds.[35]

The tension between organized labor and management did not end with the resolution of the dispute at the fairgrounds. Moreover, even relatively conservative unions, such as Local No. 50, were stigmatized in the public mind for their role in the first two strikes and for their apparent lack of public-spiritedness in the third. Nor was it any help to them that many people believed the unions (particularly the painters') to be dominated by socialists who had endorsed the construction strikes as a means of instigating class warfare.[36]

However, it is clear that the most serious confrontations were over after the fair and that the ranks of the Carpenters' Union continued to grow while the union retained its standing in the city's construction industry. As an example, in January 1904, the Master Builders' Association offered to pay the wage of $3.50 for an eight-hour day across the board to union carpenters if the union would grant the organization a monopoly of its members' skills. The union felt confident enough of the demand for its services to reject the offer.[37]

The union's expansion was remarkable. In April 1904, William Bailey, the United Brotherhood of Carpenters' organizer in the Northwest, announced that two new locals were being formed in Portland. Local No. 1673 was subsequently chartered on 28 April 1904, with forty members on its rolls. Local No. 1638 was chartered two days later. In 1905, the two consolidated as No. 1673, which shortly afterward merged with No. 50. An earlier local, No. 1450, chartered in February 1903, had disbanded in June 1904. Nevertheless, as that year began, Portland had nearly eighteen hundred union carpenters.

While membership in the union brought status and financial benefits to the craftsman, the cause of the dramatic increase was the eight-hour day. As the brotherhood's general secretary, Frank Duffy, pointed out, by the fall of 1903, shorter hours had created employment for thirty thousand more men. They had swelled the union ranks to a total of 167,229 in 1,696 locals across the nation.[38]

Even as Local No. 50 was embroiled in the strikes of 1902 and 1903, the general office was having second thoughts on the subject of militancy. In the tradition of business unionism, the national leadership strongly desired a return to a cooperative posture in its relationship with employers. With the confidence born of success and ever-increasing strength, in his annual report of 1903 Duffy called for a more conciliatory approach to the bosses. "Our policy," he wrote, "should not be one of antagonism to our employers . . . but to secure conferences with them, and through negotiations, conciliation, or arbitration, bring about satisfactory results."[39]

Local No. 50 subscribed to that policy in the same year by sponsoring an open meeting, with one of Portland's leading businessmen, Benjamin Cohen, president of the Portland Trust Company, as guest speaker. Calling unions and employers frequently unreasonable, Cohen advocated arbitration of labor disputes. The *Labor Press* praised the idea of meeting with a "capitalist and employer," and the carpenters were apparently encouraged by the contact because other such gatherings were scheduled.[40]

In 1904, in light of its renewed conservatism, its identification of its interests with its employers, and the recognition that the Federated Trades Council had become a hotbed of radicalism, Local No. 50 withdrew from the organization. Inasmuch as it was the largest union in the city and had for several years been its leading contributor, the carpenters' withdrawal was a devastating blow to the Federated Trades Council.

FOUR
Making Adjustments

IN THE FIRST TWENTY-THREE YEARS OF ITS
existence in Portland, the activities of the United Brotherhood of Carpenters and Joiners of America were
marked by almost continuous growth. By 1906, however, the upward
curve of expansion and activity had faltered. The three new locals had
expired or been subsumed by the older one after brief lives. But the carpenters of No. 50 had retained their position of leadership in the city's labor
affairs.

At the national level, the union had thrown its weight behind the
Progressive agenda. Two Progressive issues that particularly interested the
carpenters were the direct election of senators, which was designed to
break the stranglehold of the railroads and the party machines on the U.S.
Senate, and national legislation enforcing the eight-hour day. In Portland,
Elmer A. Gessil of No. 50 and D.J. Burns represented the carpenters on a
fifteen-man political committee in the city charged with developing a basic

labor platform for forthcoming elections. Gessil suggested that the group go further and form a local labor party whose candidates would carry the union platform to the city's voters.[1]

The resulting platform reflected the labor movement's concerns at the national level and their continuing focus on monopolies and on other types of labor competing with white males. It is interesting to note that the carpenters and other unions felt that the eight-hour day was important to male laborers, but that if women must work, the ten-hour day was acceptable for them.[2]

The Portland unionists' determination to make themselves heard in politics was reflected in Gessil's statement of early 1906: "We are going to get out and put some men of our own in the primaries and if they are nominated, all well and good but, if not, we will run them anyway and get out and work for them."[3] This determination was confirmed in March, when twenty-five members of the Oregon Labor party issued the party's endorsements for the April primary from Carpenters' Hall. Their greatest triumph in the election, though, was a negative one, as their condemnation of John Rand's antilabor candidacy for Congress played a role in his eventual defeat.[4]

Gessil himself announced his candidacy for the state legislature, exhorting the members of the Federated Trades Council to vote for union men rather than lawyers and professional men. Later, realizing that his chances for the office were slim, he switched his energies to a campaign for the presidency of the Federated Trades Council which the carpenters had rejoined. However, Charles Schultz, a member of the Painters' Union, won, thereby perhaps indicating the council's disapproval of the carpenters' fickleness toward it. More important, the carpenters' steadfast conservatism was repugnant to the more radical unions, which still held the Federated Trades Council in sway. Most of labor's business was being conducted by the trade sectionals, including a resurgent Building Trades Council, rather than the Federated Trades Council.[5]

The oncoming summer of 1906 found the union resuming its pattern of growth and the economic atmosphere of the city improving steadily. "The outlook for summer [building] has never been brighter," the *Labor Press* noted. "The industrial peace and quiet of the city [was] never better. For industrial felicity Portland takes a leading place."[6] Local No. 50's continued prosperity was reflected by its contribution of one hundred dollars to the San Francisco earthquake-relief fund, its vigor by the initiation of twenty-six new members in August. The resolution of a long and bitter jurisdictional dispute between the United Brotherhood of Carpenters and the British Amalgamated Society of Carpenters was also imminent and promised to strengthen the national organization. In turn, this could only have a positive impact on locals such as No. 50.

In October, the carpenters' preeminence in Portland's labor affairs was confirmed when Joseph L. Ledwidge of No. 50 was elevated to the presidency of the Federated Trades Council following the resignation of Schultz of the Painters'. Schultz's exit marked the beginning of a return to power in the struggle for control of the organiztion by the conservatives, led by the carpenters, and the decline of the radicals. From his new position, Ledwidge moved rapidly to put his own and his union's stamp on the city's labor apparatus. Under Ledwidge's direction, for example, the Federated Trades Council bought out the *Labor Press* and then changed its format. Every member of No. 50 took a subscription to the paper, which began to chronicle the carpenters' activities in minute detail.

Despite its size and power, however, Portland's United Brotherhood of Carpenters still had a fundamental problem. According to complaints by local contractors, the standard of workmanship by the city's carpenters was not uniformly high. The union, acknowledging the criticism, responded that wages in Portland were still not competitive with those of other West Coast cities, with the result that the best carpenters went elsewhere. A serious intention to improve workmanship in their projects, a union spokesman said, should begin with the contractors' improving wage scales.

Nevertheless, in the next two years, work for Portland's carpenters remained, as one official put it, "plenteous."

In May 1908, the union's general secretary, William Huber, arrived in Portland, urging a drive for expansion and better organization on the part of local carpenters. His appeal was based on the desire at the union's national headquarters for more control of the locals, somewhat reversing the philosophy by which Peter McGuire had achieved the United Brotherhood of Carpenters' early success.

When he returned to Indianapolis, Huber sent an organizer named

James Gray to Portland to begin the task. Gray, a man of tremendous energy, immediately formed a new local, designated No. 808. Actually, No. 808 was new only to Portland. The chapter had originally been chartered in Charleston, South Carolina, in 1906, but may have foundered on social or racial problems in the form of animosities between Charleston's black and mulatto carpenters. The charter was thus available for reassignment.

The *Labor Press*, awed by Gray's drive, described the episode in reverent terms. "A new era is dawning for the organized carpenters of Portland," it wrote.

> The coming of organizer J.A. Gray to the city has brought results that no one would have thought possible. The growth of the new union . . . has been at the rate of something like 40 a week and better, until the membership now is right at the 200 mark, which places the new union, of only a few weeks ago, right at the front rank with the strongest unions in the city.[7]

The officials and membership of Local No. 50, far from being jealous of their new rival, were extremely supportive of No. 808. William H. Varney, "an old union warhorse" from No. 50, switched to No. 808 to serve as its first president. The vice president, a man named Caldwell, had been a business agent in Chicago. The business agent for No. 50 agreed to serve in the same capacity for No. 808 until someone could be trained for the job. Finally, the older local sponsored the newer one for membership in the Building Trades Council.

By late June 1908, when the two locals held a joint meeting at Carpenters' Hall, membership in No. 808 had reached 225, which the *Labor Press* called "simply phenomenal for the age of the organization." The main speaker at the gathering, C.O. Young, an organizer from the national headquarters of the AFL, delivered a speech that seems to reveal why the international had moved so aggressively to establish the new local and why the members of No. 50 were so helpful in the process. The United Brotherhood of Carpenters, Young noted, was the second largest affiliated with the American Federation of Labor. If it could improve its position, the union would have great opportunities to extend its position in the craft union movement.[8]

With the support of two large and influential carpenters' locals, Young was able to accomplish his main purpose in coming to Portland, the reorganization of the Federated Trades Council. He modeled its successor, the Central Labor Council, on a structure known as the "Seattle Plan," under which the council was composed of delegates from trade sectionals as well as individual unions.

Of greater moment, perhaps, to the carpenters of Portland was the fact that the city should soon be equal in numbers of organized carpenters to Seattle, a strong union town. The national organization's strategy was to build strong regions; with Portland lagging behind other West Coast cities, the union had decided to move in. The effort was apparently well received by the carpenters of No. 50, who, like their counterparts in business, felt themselves to be competing with the growing metropolis to their north. They were, in short, Portland boosters.

Portland's carpenters were doing well, at least compared with other union members in the city. Between the two carpenters' locals, in 1908 there were approximately five hundred members, twice as many as in any other Portland union. They owned their own union hall, as well as the land on which it stood. Most of the important construction projects of the day —the Goodnough Building, the Bull Run River pipeline, and the Madison Street Bridge, for example—employed union carpenters. In addition, the chapters had acceded to the brotherhood's request for a District Council for Carpenters, consisting of five delegates from each union with a permanent secretary and a business agent, in order to foster further cooperation and coordination between the two locals. The council was to maintain complete authority locally.

By 1908, carpenters had focused clearly on the major problems they faced. The union's purposes reflect careful attention to solving these problems, as well as other goals for members of the United Brotherhood of Carpenters. As expressed in a *Labor Press* article that year, those goals were to discourage piecework; to build an apprenticeship system that would foster a higher level of skill among union carpenters; to assist fellow carpenters in finding work at fair and competitive wages in decent surroundings; and to elevate the social, intellectual, and moral life of members through discussion groups and speakers.[9]

In October 1908, when Bomberger returned to Portland from the United Brotherhood of Carpenters' national convention, he reported to the membership on significant changes in union benefits. Increases in coverage insured sickness up to forty dollars and could bring a maximum of five hundred in disability payments. A carpenter's tools could be insured against fire damage.

In 1908 carpenters could be employed as journeymen carpenters or joiners, floor layers, stair builders, ship joiners, millwrights, railcar builders, or woodworking machine operators. Full union benefits were restricted to men between twenty-one and fifty years of age, while apprentices between seventeen and twenty-one and men over fifty received only partial benefits, but in Portland as well as elsewhere, the United Brotherhood of Carpenters continued to grow. Most of the members were confident of the attractiveness of their union.

In Portland, however, subtle changes began to alter the relationships among the unions in 1909, and the carpenters seem to have lost their position as leader of the city's labor organizations. This marked the end of the two-year surge of activity characterized by the imposition by the national headquarters of greater structure and control of the locals, and also by the locals' great growth.

A tool of growth for No. 50 and No. 808 had been the close relationship both chapters enjoyed with the Portland *Labor Press*. The locals regarded the paper as their official organ and, in return, the *Labor Press* reported the carpenters' activities devotedly. If nothing else, this exposure alone must have done much to convince Portland's workingmen that the carpenters' union was one of the leading and most forward-looking labor organizations in the city.

However, after 1908, when the Central Labor Council took over the *Labor Press*, the paper ceased to cover the carpenters so assiduously. An occasional story or notice about the two locals' affairs still appeared, but the news was largely of other unions. The carpenters' fears about their strength compared with that of the various short-lived coordinating groups (the Central Labor Council was only the latest incarnation) began to be realized as the new body proved stronger and more aggressive than any of its predecessors.

Moreover, by 1909, the central labor organizations with which No. 50 and No. 808 were associated had begun to assert their own power and, therefore, to limit the freedom of action of their two carpenter affiliates. Once it returned to full strength, the Building Trades Council, for instance, represented fourteen other unions besides the carpenters. It forbade its affiliates from striking or boycotting without the approval of the entire council.[10] And the District Council of Carpenters, though composed of delegates from the two locals, was largely a creature of the national organization.

As a result, while many respected individuals of the carpenter locals, such as Bomberger and Ledwidge, continued to figure prominently in the larger organizations, the carpenters lost some of their leadership and influence in Portland's labor community. On the other hand, the members of No. 50 and No. 808 had steady work, so that this loss did not affect the members as much as it might have in harder times.[11]

Also limiting the union's influence was that, despite its proliferation of labor organizations as the new century matured, Portland had a lingering reputation as an "open-shop" town. "Would-be industrial captains," as the *Labor Press* called them in 1910, "persisted in hiring nonunion workers and the city continued to suffer under the curse of low wages."[12] The paper charged that only Los Angeles, "the city of invalids," had a lower wage level than Portland among West Coast cities, "and that doesn't count."[13]

The carpenters' locals had to keep up a constant campaign to maintain their economic advances. In 1909 the two locals sent men to work on St. Johns School on eight-hour shifts, at the prevailing union wage of $3.50. But, at the same time, they were battling the school board over the use of nonunion carpenters at the Albina High School site, where workmen received $2.75 each for nine hours' work.[14]

One strategy the locals used in the struggle was that of apprenticeship and training. Hoping to set their well-trained and experienced members apart from those who merely called themselves carpenters, and thereby to

justify the higher union wage, in 1909 No. 808 set up a Training Department to teach courses in carpentry and joining. An education committee
was charged with the task of finding texts on the use of the carpenter's
square, the steel square, plans, specifications, and blueprints.[15]

Such efforts, coupled with the carpenters' reputation, kept the United Brotherhood of Carpenters of Portland growing. A year-end report of
1909 noted 626 members in good standing for the combined locals.[16] Local
No. 50 was forced to commission two new business agents to deal with the
membership growth, which had not abated although some of the rank and
file had left the union over the issue of excessive centralization. The agents,
Calvin Ziegler and John H. Andrews, solicited new members, contacted
lapsed ones, and pressured contractors to hire union carpenters.

Still, the open shop persisted, weakening Portland's construction unions in general and the carpenters in particular. Indeed, because of its
effects, the carpenters finally saw some of their affiliation in the central
groups. A letter circulated to members of both No. 50 and No. 808 in 1909
suggested that a major step in combating the open shop in their own trade
was to assist in the unionization of others, "through organization of the
Building Trades," in order to protect the workingmen against the "tyranny
and greed of organized capital."[17]

A major struggle took shape in 1909-10 over the open-shop principle.
The Olds, Wortman, and King Department Store construction site was
boycotted by the Building Trades Council as well as the Central Labor
Council for the use of nonunion labor by the contractor. Meanwhile,
other contractors, such as the Northwest Bridge Company, Hurley and
Mason, and Reed and McKinnon, who were judged recalcitrant or unfair
were put on the unfair list. They and other uncooperative employers, according to the *Labor Press*, had "raised hell with the trades," through the
open shop. The carpenters sent out warnings to their delinquent members
about these employers, stating that it was "up to the carpenters to refuse
unfair conditions—the contractors are forcing us to unite."[18] The show of
strength and resolve paid off in the department-store case, as the store
owners eventually came to the bargaining table.

In 1910, Portland's union carpenters found themselves in a favorable
position relative to their own economic status at the end of the nineteenth

century and to that of other Portland unions of the day. Their membership rolls remained crowded, their treasuries were full, and their prestige among the other labor organizations was reasonably secure.

Yet the open shop in the building trades continued to work against them, and their own great numbers played a part in keeping carpenters' wages at about the average level for local unions for eight hours. Other smaller locals in the building trades got better wages in 1910, merely because of supply and demand. A brief survey of Portland's labor market and the buying power of the dollar gives some indication of the economic situation for locals No. 50 and No. 808. Portland's carpenters could still expect $3.50 for the hard-won eight-hour day. Painters and electricians also received that wage, but structural iron workers were paid $4.50 for eight hours, plumbers and steamfitters $5.00, while plasterers and tile setters got $5.50.[19] In other trades, a barber in Portland earned an average of $16.00 per week, cigar makers $3.50 per day, longshoremen $4.95 for a nine- to ten-hour day. Teamsters earned $2.75 for up to eleven hours of work, a waitress $9.00 for a week of ten-hour days. A waiter could earn up to $12.50 a week, working from ten to twelve hours. A printer earned $5.00 for as few as seven hours a day.

At the same time, the costs of some dietary staples, of some ordinary hard goods, and of some basic building materials were as follows in 1910: apples—$.08 per pound, beef—$.15 per pound, coffee—$.20 per pound, eggs—$.30 per dozen, iron—$.0025 per pound, rough lumber—$14.00 per thousand, nails—$.04 per pound. A cooking stove cost $30.00.

In the circumstances, the carpenters' locals could not relax in their pursuit of improved wages and conditions. That year, Portland sent representatives to a meeting of the Northwest Council of Carpenters, an organization arising from the brotherhood's plan for greater control of local and regional affairs. The meeting was called to design a plan to "develop a general supervision of carpenter work in the Northwest."[20] In addition to the tighter rein on the locals that this extended district council would enjoy, it was designed to enhance the power of locals engaged in strikes and boycotts.

Locals No. 50 and No. 808 also continued to participate actively in the Building Trades Council. The council, by 1910 a sophisticated body, began sending a business agent to each of the districts into which it had recently divided the city, as part of its plan to scrutinize the activities of its member groups. In another instance of this increased sophistication, the council adopted a card-index system that provided statistics on the members of the carpenters' locals.[21] In addition, the more conservative unions, such as the carpenters, maintained a tighter grip on the council's activities, particularly after the restriction of 1909 on strikes and boycotts by individual unions.

On the other hand, the building trades had not been altogether in control of construction jobs (as the carpenters' concern over the open shop illustrates) since the strikes of 1902 and 1903, and sometimes the council therefore pressed too hard to regain its lost power quickly. To combat open-shop contractors, the Building Trades Council had initiated a large number of boycotts of nonunion buildings. Besides the fact that they had a negligible effect on the contractors and the commerce associated with the buildings, the boycotts succeeded only in antagonizing public opinion and somewhat demoralizing the unions.

Part of the problem was the inconsistency with which the boycotts were applied. For instance, in 1911 the Building Trades Council, in contrast with its handling of the Olds, Wortman, and King job, ignored the construction of two buildings by nonunion labor, yet boycotted all the businesses in them after they opened their doors. The *Labor Press*, incredulous, asked if the issue were to be settled by razing the offending buildings.[22]

The Central Labor Council, meanwhile, had likewise grown in power and stature, to the extent that by early 1911, the *Labor Press* could call it a "big factor" in Portland's labor movement.[23] This development of union bureaucracy indicates the extent to which the local labor movement had become a complex structure of interlocking interests and power. It also shows how the original autonomy of the carpenters' locals had become greatly restricted since 1883. The trade-off was the ensuing increase in strength of the combined locals.

FIVE
The Problems of Peace and War

DESPITE THE INCREASED ENERGY OF
Portland carpenters and the other building trades unions
around 1909, organized labor continued to experience
difficulties. Downward trends in the city's economy caused concern, as the
carpenters remained convinced that unionists were being displaced by the
increasing immigration to Oregon from other states, over which they had
no discernible control.[1]

More worrying, however, was the attitude of Portland's employers
and politicians toward labor. At the decade's end, employers formed an
association which some called a response specifically to the "foolish and
boisterous" boycotts of the Building Trades Council. The main purpose of
the organization seems to have been to curtail union activity. Most alarm-
ing to the unions was that the mayor and city council were highly receptive
to the association's lobbying. In 1910 the council passed an ordinance that
forbade carrying banners on city streets. An antipicketing ordinance was

passed. Two years later, the Employers' Association made extensive efforts to restrict union activities even more drastically. The council actually passed many of the association's suggested pieces of legislation, but the courts quickly struck most of them down as unconstitutional.[2]

For all their problems, the unions, particularly the carpenters', continued to grow. Between 1912 and 1914, no fewer than nine new carpenter locals were chartered in Portland. In February 1912, No. 1120, a millmen's local, was chartered. This was a signal event for Portland's union carpenters. For the first time, it indicated to the city the flexibility and adaptability the United Brotherhood of Carpenters was showing, under General President William Huber, to the rapid pace of technological change. The inclusion of millmen, pile drivers, bridge builders, shipwrights, railcar builders, coffin makers, stair builders, caulkers, and others, in the same union with carpenters and joiners, made the United Brotherhood of Carpenters a hybrid—a craft-industrial union—that Peter McGuire might have been unable to recognize.

In March 1913, No. 1937, a hardwood-floor-layers' local, was chartered. On 6 May 1913, No. 583, a general-construction local, received its charter. Local No. 583, the first president of which was Max Ohm, was organized in North Portland in recognition of the growth of St. Johns, Kenton, Linnton, and the northeast quadrant in general. The carpenters of No. 583 met at the Arbor Lodge Fire Station on Portland Boulevard, near the Greeley Street intersection.[3]

Fourteen days after No. 583 officially began operating, Local No. 1106, another general-construction local, began functioning in Portland's southeastern area of Woodstock. A caulker's local, No. 1052, was born in October 1913. Local No. 1266, serving the Sellwood district, was also active in the city at the time.[4]

On 15 December 1913, two new locals indicative, as the millmen had been, of the United Brotherhood of Carpenters' expanded horizons were chartered. One, No. 872, was a bridge-, dock-, and pier-builders' local. (It would disband in 1916.) The other was No. 1020, made up of shipwrights and joiners. This group may have descended from an old shipwrights' local which was one of Portland's earlier unions, although never affiliated with the United Brotherhood of Carpenters.[5] Local No. 1020 met at Bricklayers' Hall, 272 Madison Street. One of its first officers was Charles Gregory, secretary. As an early and highly skilled craft union, the shipwrights enjoyed great prestige in labor circles. Yet their ranks were small in the best of times and their craft was changing rapidly with the rise of metal materials and the obsolescence of wooden sailing vessels. These were making shipwrights into industrial workers rather than "mechanics." Thus they never had much power in the city's organized-labor community.[6]

In January 1914, Local No. 2543 was chartered. It is not clear what its original purpose was, but in 1924 it was assigned a new number, No. 2154, and had a membership of lathers.

In 1913 wages for general carpentry were still at $3.50, although a few men were beginning to make $4.00 per day. The initiation fee was $15.00; dues were $1.00 each month.[7] Local No. 583 met each Wednesday evening; a fine of $.25 was levied if a member did not attend one meeting a month. A per-capita tax went to the general office.[8]

Meanwhile, at the national level, the United Brotherhood of Carpenters continued to gain strength. In 1914 a twelve-year jurisdictional battle with the much smaller Amalgamated Society of Carpenters was drawing to a close, as the society agreed to turn complete control over trade matters to the United Brotherhood of Carpenters. The settlement would make the latter the preeminent carpenters' organization in North America.

In March the same year, the United Brotherhood of Carpenters took another important step when it withdrew from the Building Trades Department of the AFL as the result of a dispute with the sheet-metal workers. As the national organization did not request that the various locals take similar action at the state level, this was regarded as an indication by the locals, including those in Portland, that greater latitude was being given them in setting policy and managing their own affairs.

For the Portland locals, this meant a boost in their own importance in labor circles. Indeed, they had become among the most influential unions in the region's labor affairs. In 1914, for example, three men from No. 808 assumed important posts in the Northwest District Council of the United Brotherhood of Carpenters. Ralph O. Rector was elected president, John F. Weatherby was made financial secretary, and Will Shugart was named to the executive board.

The carpenters continued to pursue a Progressive political agenda. A legislative committee representing Oregon's seventeen hundred union carpenters provided the state's United Brotherhood of Carpenters members with an analysis of a broad range of issues designed to ensure the "defeat of the enemies of labor and progress" in the 1914 primary. In January 1914 Local No. 1266 of Sellwood sponsored an address by a suffragist who considered the question "Woman and the Ballot."

The meetings of the locals had become a mixture of union business matters, political discussion, and working class gaiety. At one winter meeting in 1914, a troupe of actors from the Baker Theater in Portland afforded a memorable evening. "Nothing like it has been attempted in Local union circles," the *Labor Press* reported.

At the close of the year, the *Labor Press* published a social note that was an indication of both the morale and the history of the carpenters in Portland. Carey W. "Old Dad" Ryan, as the newspaper referred to the elderly activist of No. 50, now retired, was seen playing checkers contentedly during a gala at Carpenters' Hall while the festivities swirled around him. His comfortable, secure, declining years had been made possible by the social and economic gains made by the union in his lifetime while he represented a thirty-one-year bridge between the union's modest beginnings in Portland in 1883 and the well-established organization of the early twentieth century.

Of more significance, however, was the 1914 Labor Day issue of the *Labor Press*, which displayed pictures of the Northwestern National Bank in Portland, the police headquarters, the Platt, Stevens, and Yeon buildings (at its dedication, the Yeon Building was Portland's tallest), the Multnomah County Courthouse, the Madison Street Bridge, various theaters, and other landmarks of the city, all of which had been constructed by members of the carpenter locals. It was an impressive catalogue, not only of the city's growth, but of the labor of the men who had achieved that growth with their own hands. More pointedly, each structure was a symbol of the reasonable hours on the job, at dignified wages, that made the union a vital part of the economic and social fabric of the city itself.

The union's attainments were glowingly enumerated in an article commemorating the Brotherhood's thirty-four-year anniversary. Frank

Duffy, general secretary of the United Brotherhood of Carpenters, spoke to the national record of the union, but his words stood for the accomplishments of Portland's carpenter locals as well. "We have done much good in our time," he wrote. "We have relieved our members of the burdens that pressed heavily upon them; we have established better working conditions; we have fought for better homes to live in and better shops to work in; we have visited the sick and buried the dead; we have demanded a better education for our children. . . . We are proud of our record."[9]

Nevertheless, the carpenters' energy, self-confidence, and economic well-being at both national and local levels continued to be threatened by economic tension, internecine discord, and the chronically adverse public image of unions. Among other things, it was becoming apparent to the national office of the United Brotherhood of Carpenters that the proliferating Portland locals were so competitive among themselves that the union's growth and its progress in the battle against the carpenters' true adversary, the nonunion employer, were being impeded. In 1915, in the course of a national tour, William Hutcheson, national vice president, bluntly told Portland's carpenters, in a speech at Carpenters' Hall, to eliminate the "petty jealousy" that was paralyzing the locals and get on with the job of organizing the city's craftsmen.[10]

In addition, the local economy was in the doldrums. Accordingly, the officials of No. 50 and No. 808, in a joint appeal to employers, noted that unemployment in the city was so high that the business community should halt its boosterism and encouragement of immigration to the state, which only succeeded in increasing competition for the dwindling pool of available jobs.[11] The usual pleas for out-of-state workmen to stay away from Oregon filled Portland's reports to *The Carpenter* magazine at the same time.

Meanwhile, a wider gulf than usual opened between the Northwest labor movement as a whole and the general public in their respective views of issues of the day. The *Labor Press* seemed constantly at loggerheads with the *Oregonian*, a case in point being the treatment by the authorities of the Industrial Workers of the World (IWW), better known as the "Wobblies." While hardly sympathetic to the Wobblies' revolutionary agenda, the *Labor Press* and the unions it represented were inclined to agree with the IWW that their rights of free speech and assembly had been abused in various notorious clashes with the police and state militias. Labor, therefore, defended the Wobblies. The *Oregonian*, on the other hand, viewed the IWW as a menace to society and consistently applauded the use of the harshest measures against its members.

By the same token, Portland's labor leaders frequently indulged in intemperate rhetorical attacks on their opponents in the business and political communities. An anti-union attitude, for example, earned Simon Benson, a Norwegian by birth, and one of the state's leading citizens, the Central Labor Council's suggestion that he be deported.[12]

If such views ran counter to the general tide of public sentiment, a worse problem was taking shape for labor. The Great War in Europe, which had been raging since August 1914, thoroughly engaged public attention in the United States by the next year. While there was sharp and extended debate over the merits of American involvement until the nation's actual entry into the war in 1917, a martial sensibility came over even avowed neutralists. Organized labor, meantime, spoke out against the military and the militia. The unions, whose history was studded with incidents involving the use of troops against them, distrusted the military and its apologists. Portland's labor members were so touchy on the subject of military preparedness that the Oregon State Federation of Labor at one point denounced the Boy Scouts, who were touring the nation and stirring patriotic emotions with the Liberty Bell.[13] As public opinion across the United States responded ever more belligerently to feverish but convincing reports by the highly effective British propaganda machine of German depredations against neutrals, such outbursts did nothing to improve labor's profile in the community.

Early in 1916, the competition and organizational confusion among Portland's carpenters' locals was mitigated when, after an autumn of preliminary discussions and negotiations, locals No. 50 and No. 808 merged. On 8 February, the new local met and elected a slate of officers, including Truman Bentley, president; Charles Woodward, vice president; Sylvester T. Clark, financial secretary; and W.A. Weaver, recording secretary. Bert Sleeman, an energetic young man who had begun to make a name for himself as an organizer, remained as business agent of the new local, after having held the position in No. 808 since 1907.[14] On 1 April, the new local, which had remained No. 50, became No. 226.

In June 1916, there was a change of leadership for No. 226, when Glenn Harris became president. Apart from this, everything about the formation of No. 226 led to resolution of the disorder among Portland's carpenters' locals. The new body was one of the largest (if not the largest) carpenters' locals in the state. Many of its members represented a direct link to the city's first labor movement of consequence. The tradition and standing they brought to No. 226, coupled with the large membership (no figures are available, but it is safe to assume that there were over nine hundred), made it the preeminent local in Portland, in charge of dispatching workmen for the central city on both sides of the Willamette River. The other locals were largely reduced to satellite status, with purview over outlying communities, neighborhoods, or suburbs, as in the case of No. 1106 in Sellwood and No. 583 in Kenton, or over a particular subspecialty of the craft, as in the case of No. 1020, the shipwrights' local.

Even as the carpenters got their house in order, world events were transforming the city's economy and narrowing the differences between its unionized and nonunion citizens. The United States' entrance into the Great War had, by 1916, become virtually a certainty. As early as July 1915, President Woodrow Wilson had told the Armed Services to plan for their imminent expansion while he worked hard to maintain the nation's neutrality. While most of the public earnestly desired that he should, the American economy began preparing for war. This led to a steady expansion of the country's industrial capacity, and therefore of jobs. At first, most of the increased output went to the Allied Powers—England, France, and Italy—but, eventually, as U.S. belligerence became more likely, it started flowing to the American military.

The impact of war-related production on Portland had begun to be felt as early as 1914 in the shipbuilding industry, when contracts were let for some vessels to be built by the city's respected ship-construction industry. The orders were for wooden merchantmen, not warships, and the customers were private. By November 1916, however, a genuine shipbuilding boom was occurring on the banks of the Willamette and Columbia rivers. The Chamber of Commerce announced that in that month $21 million in contracts had been awarded to Portland's shipyards.[15] When the United States entered the conflict on 6 April 1917, the yards were working to capacity. By the end of hostilities in 1918, there were orders for 154 wooden ships and 102 steel ships.[16]

In the strange way of war, the agony of some was the opportunity of others. The wooden ship, only recently giving up the sea lanes to the steel hull, enjoyed a renaissance because it offered relatively cheap and quick construction. Portland's yards were the logical choice. The *Labor Press*, having voiced the unions' frustrations over the prolonged sluggishness in the construction markets, trumpeted their glee. "'Ships, give us ships,' was the sad petition of the shippers." Oregon stumbled on the answer, said the paper. "The ships were growing on the banks."[17] And not only the ships, the planes were there too: lumber would win the war.[18] For Portland's labor, trees meant jobs.

The evidence of the shipbuilding boom soon became apparent on the streets of Portland. Would-be shipwrights and other construction workers descended on the city like locusts. Farmers, small-town carpenters, and transients arrived on their own, and the construction companies imported "thousands" of others.[19] The major yards in the city—Northwest Steel, Willamette Iron and Steel, Albina Shipbuilding and Machine Company, Smith & Watson Iron Works, Grant Smith-Porter, Columbia River Shipbuilding Company, and Supple & Ballin—ran at full capacity and required large contingents of workers. Indeed, some of the yards ran far beyond their prewar capacity. Northwest had barely existed in 1916, but by 1917 it had gone from almost no capacity to twelve acres of ways and shops, from which it sent forty-two ships into the Willamette.[20]

For the carpenters' locals, as for organized labor generally, jobs were only a part of their improved position from war. There were also new members for the unions. Local No. 226 had a membership increase of 125 in one five-week period in late August and early September 1917 alone.[21] Local No. 1020, the one most identified with shipbuilding, rose to a membership over one thousand by 1918. During the meeting on 10 February 1918 alone, eighty-five new members were initiated.[22] The clamor for admission had grown to such proportions that special initiation meetings had to be held and larger quarters had to be sought for general business meetings.[23] The local began to meet in Auditorium Hall, between Third and Taylor in the business district.

The war helped to heal the breach between the unions and the public. The surge of patriotism that inevitably accompanied the United States' entry swept over the unions, and while they never became avid supporters of the conflict or participants in the occasional outbursts of xenophobic hysteria the war brought on, organized labor contributed to the war effort in a sedate way. Members of Local No. 583, for example, by late 1918 had sold ten thousand dollars worth of Liberty Bonds, on their way to a goal of fifty thousand.[24] In any case, the carpenters could claim during the war to be more in the mainstream of the community's life than at any time in the previous decade.

The carpenters working on Portland's wooden vessels during the Great War may not have realized it, but they were participating in perhaps the final surge of construction of wooden ships in the United States. Clearly, they were thus to enjoy the last major opportunity to practice the ancient craft of the shipwright.

In 1918 the federal contracting agency, the United States Shipping Board, Emergency Fleet Corporation, with unintended irony released a manual for its personnel officers. The manual broke down the tasks of shipbuilding into discrete jobs that made a painstaking handcraft sound like so many aspects of mass production. Nevertheless, the job descriptions preserve, like the artifacts in a Pharaoh's tomb, the essence of carpentry's most arduous, complex, and esoteric craft, even as it passed from the industrial landscape.

Under "trade requirements" for a ship carpenter, the manual gave a comprehensive description:

> He must be a skilled all-around Ship Carpenter and be familiar with the construction of the ship from the laying of the keel until the vessel is finished. The work consists of building foundations, erecting and truing the ways in which the ship is to be constructed, laying keel blocks, setting up shores, setting backings for the riveters, laying wooden decks, installing ceilings, and preparing the ship for launching, laying off and installing deck fittings, gun foundations,

auxiliary machinery foundations, etc., and keeping the ship fair upon the ways. He should be capable of bevelling and dubbing. Bevelling is the matching of planking or timbers before they are placed in a position on the ship by cutting such material to the proper angle. Dubbing is the trimming done on the planking or timbers after they are placed in position. This work is done with an adz or pneumatic trimmer.[25]

A ship carpenter needed to be a master carpenter, highly experienced and universally knowledgeable in the craft. He had to be able to read all kinds of blueprints.[26] A planker did the following: "after the frame of the vessel has been placed and the dubbers have smoothed the timbers, the Plankers 'stick' the planks on the hull by boring, driving and wedging trunnels, and later fasten the planks with spikes. They also lay the decks, fastening them with bolts, drift pins or screws."[27]

Experience as a dock builder or bridge builder, or in heavy carpentry, was regarded as desirable preparation for plankers.[28] A squarer followed the plankers to "fair up the surfaces" with an adz and a broadax.[29]

A reamer drove with a beedle (a wide flat iron also known as a "horsing iron") into the seams between the planks in the hull and on the deck to open them for the entrance of an oakum caulking compound. His was chiefly a repairman's role.[30] He was expected to be adept at working in "different postures."[31]

A sparmaker finished and installed "square, octagonal, and round spars, masts, cargo booms, etc.," and "applied . . . [their] fittings."[32] A stage builder was a rough carpenter who built scaffolding.[33]

Joiners followed their own time-honored specialty, doing the interiors of ships, making and hanging doors, windows, cabinets, desks, instrument cases, and so forth.[34]

The shipbuilder's craft was encouraged at the time with night training courses offered by the Federal Board of Vocational Training in cooperation with the Oregon State Board.[35]

The Portland shipyards themselves were generally productive and efficient from the outset of the wartime production period. The Grant Smith-Porter yard was regarded by the Emergency Shipping Board as one of the most distinguished in the nation. In its yearbook for 1919, the board wrote, "the performance of this yard heads the list among wood shipbuilding yards of the century."[36] With union carpenters Bert Pettitt, general foreman; H.J. Carlson, framing foreman; and Elmer Hanson, ship foreman, the north ways crew of Grant Smith-Porter set a world record for ship framing by building twenty-two frames in eight hours (the old record was sixteen; eight was considered good). In the same week, the same crew established another record by enclosing an entire hull in six days.[37]

As a whole, the Portland yards broke all previous production records in August 1918 for the delivery of new ships. In that month, the city's shipyards produced sixty-six ships, totaling 340,145 deadweight tons.[38]

The feverish pace of wartime production, with its concomitant full employment—in the minutes of Central Labor Council meetings, the report of the Building Trades was usually a simple but pregnant phrase: "everybody working"—nonetheless masked problems in the industry that affected the carpenters greatly. For one thing, the wage differential between shipyards in Portland and elsewhere was highly unfavorable. In 1917, a Portland shipwright received $5.60 per day, but master carpenters were being offered as much as $8.00 per day by out-of-state employers.

Portland's marine wage structure was low because there were many open-shop companies in the city. The open shop, in fact, prevailed nationwide in the shipyards, causing continuing friction between the building trades, whose services were obviously crucial to the war effort, and the War Department, under Secretary Newton D. Baker, over the open-shop policy in government projects.[39] The government took the position that a vast number of workers would need to be recruited and trained to fuel the furious pace of construction. The closed shop, it maintained, would only retard this process and thus impede the war effort. Naturally, the government also assumed that unionization would drive up the cost of labor on the war projects.

The AFL, under Gompers, and the United Brotherhood of Carpenters, under the leadership of William L. "Big Bill" Hutcheson—as forceful a personality as the American labor movement ever produced—pressed hard and incessantly for some sort of agreement on the closed shop, particularly for the shipyards. Many old-line yards were well managed, but the war had also brought entrepreneurs and profiteers into the shipbuilding business. As a result, there were many yards on both coasts, on the Great Lakes, and on the Gulf Coast, run by neophytes and fly-by-nights, in which inefficiency, low wages, and poor (when not outright dangerous) working conditions prevailed.

Gompers had earlier signed an agreement with Baker for the union scale on government projects, in return, in effect, for the open shop. While it is not clear that Gompers understood the import of his action, and while the agreement for the most part worked well in regular construction, it was a disaster for shipbuilding labor and, in any case, unacceptable to Hutcheson. The carpenters' president had his own aggressive view of labor's role in the war effort, as well as the only comprehensive plan for effecting it, but with the government clinging to the Gompers-Baker accord, he had a continuing battle on his hands. The result was that Portland's shipyard labor was only one part of a nationwide pattern of tension and confrontation.

The city's metal trades (unions involved in ship construction, including the shipwrights of Local No. 1020) were so frustrated by these mutually reinforcing occurrences that they planned "the biggest strike in Portland history" for 10:00 A.M. on 22 April 1917.[40] With confrontation in the air only a few days after the United States had entered the war (6 April), the federal government rushed a mediator in to pacify the unionists. After extended talks with both sides, the mediator held a meeting for labor at Municipal Auditorium in late August. It was attended by twenty-five hundred members of the metal trades unions. The mediator, a man named George Y. Harry, said that the government had commandeered the output of the yards as a consequence of the nation's entrance into the war.[41] The Emergency Shipping Board had thus assumed jurisdiction over shipyard labor relations and would decide the union's wage and hour claims. Harry pleaded for patience until the government could study the issue. Union leaders and rank-and-file members alike promised to postpone the strike pending a government decision on their wages. They insisted, however, on the closed shop as a nonnegotiable aspect of any settlement.[42]

Earlier in the year, two yards, Willamette Iron and Steel and Northwest Steel, had been struck over helpers' wages and the closed shop. The companies had hired strikebreakers who lived on a barge in the river, but had eventually been forced to settle when many of the most skilled of the idled workers, including some shipwrights, were lured away to yards in other cities by promises of much higher pay. The employers had thus been forced to deal with the Metal Trades Council, an organization that had arisen out of the growth of construction crafts working primarily in metal materials, which they had previously refused to do. On the other hand, they had vowed never to accept the closed shop, thereby ensuring continued strife.[43]

As a result of Harry's pacification efforts, the Metal Trades Council sent two representatives, a machinist and a blacksmith, to Washington, D.C., to state the union's case to the Emergency Shipping Board. There, they continued to press for the closed shop, as well as the packages of the individual crafts. For the carpenters in the wooden shipbuilding yards, this meant a minimum hourly wage of $.70 for an eight-hour day; double-time pay for overtime, including Saturday afternoons, Sundays, and holidays; pay to be drawn every Saturday; and no deduction from pay for hospital fees.[44]

By comparison, the general-construction carpenters had negotiated a contract with their employers, effective 15 September 1917, that featured a seventy cent minimum hourly wage and an eight-to-five workday, with all work to cease at noon Saturday, and the period from Saturday noon to Monday at 8:00 A.M. to be compensated at double time.[45] Overtime was not to be sanctioned except in cases of extreme necessity, and then only with a permit from the District Council of Carpenters. Double time was also to be paid for the Fourth of July, Decoration Day, Thanksgiving Day, Christmas Day, and days of national and state elections. There would be no work on Labor Day, and when a holiday fell on a Sunday, the following Monday was to be observed.[46]

The tense atmosphere in Portland's shipyards was ignited by news of a lockout of workers at the McEachern and Wilson yards in Astoria. According to reports, the men had been told on Friday, 15 September, that there was no work until Monday, but not to return on that day as union members.[47] Although no violence resulted, the governor of Oregon, James Withycombe, had ordered troops of the Oregon National Guard to Astoria.[48]

The confrontation soon spread upriver through the shipyards of the Columbia and the Willamette. By the end of the month, some eight thousand men were on strike. All yards, both wood and steel, were affected. Strangely, in light of the national emergency and the ever-growing strength of the unions in boom times, the u.s. Wage Adjustment Board, the hearings agency of the government, and the shipyard owners did not seem concerned about settling the dispute. The government delayed answering queries submitted by the unions and the employers simply refused to deal with the union negotiators.[49] Because the major issue of the dispute was the closed shop, management perhaps believed too much was at stake to act hastily. It may also have felt confident that the war fever of the times, accompanied by dramatic gestures such as Withycombe's, on the part of the state and local authorities, would cast labor in an unpatriotic light and cause the unions to capitulate without an extended fight.

Although the portly, opportunistic mayor of Portland, George Baker, met with the shipyard employers and subsequently ordered the police to enforce the city's controversial anticonspiracy ordinance against strikers, the unions did not have much time to feel public disapproval. Following hearings with the shipbuilding Wage Adjustment Board, in October all the strikers returned to work. The unions felt that the settlement negotiated by the board gave them everything they had asked for, including the closed shop.[50] Their confidence in the establishment of the closed shop rested on a passage from Part 8 of the settlement: "So far as practicable and where men are available, all labor in connection with construction work and repairs, shall be done by employees in the trades or calling generally recognized as having jurisdiction therein."[51]

The tranquillity expected to result from the settlement did not develop. On the surface, production went forward unimpeded. Governor Withycombe maintained that there was "no dissatisfaction among shipyard workers as far as I know."[52] Yet the *Labor Press* claimed to have documented proof that men were receiving from $.25 to $2.00 a day less than the Wage Adjustment Board's settlement had authorized.[53] The paper declared that dissatisfaction prevailed among workers and that therefore it was only a matter of time before another strike resulted.

Increased production and tension marked most of 1918, but if labor-management relations were unstable, two additional difficulties soon emerged. The first was the government's apparent view that the wooden ship was obsolete. As World War I drew to a close, the Emergency Fleet Corporation, operators of the wartime merchant marine for the Emergency Shipping Board, were disenchanted with the economics of wooden vessels. There had been experiments with alternatives, such as the cement hull, but they were not successful. On the other hand, government spokesmen hinted that the building of wooden ships was doomed.

Just before the Armistice on 11 November 1918, Charles Piez, general manager of the Emergency Fleet Corporation, announced that a "revision" of the government's policy with regard to wooden vessels would be made.[54] He hinted darkly that any changes might be accompanied by layoffs at the yards. Then, on Monday, 21 November, the u.s. Shipping Board announced cancellation of all contracts for wooden ships except those already under construction.[55] The leadership of the shipbuilding industry on the West Coast, both management and labor, predicted that the new policy would seriously hurt the West Coast economy and throw several thousand men out of work.

The second problem, of which the wooden-ship policy was merely an aspect, was that the war was over in fact if not by treaty by the fall of 1918. The government was definitely not going to need wooden ships; neither would it need most of the steel vessels still on back order.

Layoffs in shipbuilding began almost immediately after the Armistice was signed. Some men had been let go even before the coming of peace. The carpenters and other unions made efforts to keep men at work and to prepare the industry in Portland for a peacetime economy in which shipbuilding would continue under favorable circumstances for labor. A mass meeting of shipyard workers held at the Public Auditorium, for example, was for the purpose of discussing the transition. Meanwhile Otto Hartwig, president of the Oregon State Federation of Labor, met with the executive board of the AFL to urge it to use its influence with Congress and the Shipping Board to save the building of wooden ships.[56] Earlier, the

Columbia River District Maritime Council and the Portland Metal Trades Council had voted for the forty-four-hour week to provide work for more men in the face of the widening pattern of layoffs.[57]

In the meantime, an automatic increase had gone into effect for the yards. The shipbuilding Wage Adjustment Board had guaranteed a large raise for the lowest-paid workers, based on advances in the cost of living. While the less skilled men were getting an increase of some 20 percent, journeymen and skilled workers received nothing so large. Carpenters received an increase of less than 7 percent.

Despite the precarious position of the member unions with respect to employment in shipbuilding, the Pacific Coast Metal Trades Council rejected the pay raise and planned to appeal the board's decision.[58] The government, anxious to avert further negotiations and the possibility of higher wages, terminated the shipbuilding Wage Adjustment Board in early 1919.[59] Portland shipyard owners, meanwhile, cognizant of the need to keep their plants working at full speed in order to avoid cancellation of remaining contracts, agreed to a wage increase with the Metal Trades Council. The Emergency Fleet Corporation, fearing a precedent that might spread to yards throughout the nation, refused to allow the increment to be figured into its contracts with the yards. The desperate owners, however, agreed to pay the increase out of their own pockets.[60]

In other cities along the West Coast, a full-scale strike had broken out as a result of the refusal of the government and the shipyard owners to cooperate with labor. Two recalcitrant yards in Portland were also struck with some violence, but the city enjoyed relative calm overall. In 1920, the government allowed ninety-seven additional ships to be built with the increased wage figured in the contracts.

Yet the reality was that, with the Armistice, the shipbuilding boom was over for Portland. Almost overnight, once-busy yards went back to their normal prewar iron and steel projects. Others, lacking a peacetime business, fell into disrepair. Still others, such as the Northwest Steel Yards and the Grant Smith-Porter Company, were dismantled and sold for scrap. Most of the workers filtered back to farms, villages, and factories. The last steel cargo ship of the war years to be built in Portland was the *Clauseus*, launched from Northwest Steel Yards, 5 December 1919.[61]

The solidarity of the shipbuilding unions during the war had an effect on the carpenters of Local No. 1020, for they identified their interests with the maritime unions and the metal trades, rather than with the carpenters. Bert Sleeman, the District Council business agent, struck an agreement with Local No. 1020 in the spring of 1918, allowing its members to carry the Pacific Coast Maritime Council card and wear its button while still remaining in the United Brotherhood of Carpenters. Then, in September 1919, the local, with other West Coast shipyard carpenters' locals, left the United Brotherhood of Carpenters in an attempt to be recognized by the AFL as a separate shipwrights' union.[62] Some arm-twisting by Hutcheson, however, convinced Local No. 1020 to reaffiliate with the United Brotherhood of Carpenters. Through his persuasion, the members understood that their best interest lay with the carpenters' union, the strongest craft organization in the United States.

During the second decade of the twentieth century, the life of a carpenter in Portland was arduous. Art N. Vail, a member of No. 226, characterized the difficulties and frustrations of the journeyman in 1917 in a poem reprinted in the *Labor Press*. The sardonic tenor of his view is captured in a few stanzas from "A Carpenter's Dream."

Last night as I lay sleeping,
    I heard the falling of a mighty bell;
I dreamed that I cashed in my check
    And was on my road to h—l.

I walked up to a palace,
    But I found it hard to pass,
For the doorkeeper informed me
    That it was for the better class.

When I asked him about construction
    He seemed to be quite clever.
He said the work here never stops,
    But goes right on forever.

Then I spied a unique figure,
    Higher up on the level.
It was the chief architect
    Better known as the devil.

He said, "You are a weary looking creature;
    A few years ago you were stout;
You have carried tools upon your back
    Until they wore you out.

"When you went to the hardware store
    And bought your first kit of tools,
You thought you were entering a great business,
    But you were joining an army of fools.

"Carpenters do not enter here,
    For much they are not worth,
So go right up to heaven,
    For you have had your hell on earth."[63]

SIX
Breathing Room: Prosperity, Cooperation, Adaptation

AMERICA SETTLED INTO THE 1920S IN A conservative mood. The election of the Republican Warren G. Harding to the presidency in 1920, the elevation of business and businessmen to a preferred status in American life, and a growing isolationism all gave evidence of this trend. However, on a national level, with some exceptions, the American labor movement persisted in the mainstream of Progressivism.

In Portland, a lingering anti-Asian bias remained among West Coast workingmen, while local unions were largely tolerant of other foreigners and supported progressive candidates for political office. When the *Oregonian* wrung its hands editorially over the presence of Russian immigrants and what it viewed as other likely radicals of foreign descent in Portland, the *Labor Press* condemned the witch-hunt atmosphere of the times.[1] This view was understandable, in that a sizable minority of the area's skilled union craftsmen, particularly among the carpenters, were themselves recent immigrants or first-generation Americans. There was such a high proportion of Scandinavians among Portland's carpenters, for example, that it was said you couldn't be a carpenter unless your name ended with "son."[2] In the shipyards, a certain operation on the construction of barges requiring eight-inch spikes to be driven through six-inch overhead beams was commonly said to be accomplished through "Swede power."[3]

Organized labor continued to support strong legislation curbing immigration, probably from a chronic fear of an influx of unorganized workers who would drive their members out of the market. On at least one occasion during the shipyard strikes of the war years, a rumor that Chinese workmen were seen carrying their own tools into a struck shipyard caused great consternation among the union men.

The tension between their libertarianism and their isolationism did not dampen the enthusiasm of the unions, particularly the carpenters, for mainstream political candidates. In the 1920 presidential primary in Oregon, the *Labor Press*, speaking for the Oregon State Federation of Labor and the carpenters, endorsed the doughty California Progressive, Hiram Johnson, and ridiculed Harding, the eventual winner.[4] Next to Johnson, the editors said bluntly, Harding was an idiot.

On a more mundane level, the unions in general and the carpenters in particular continued to become more deeply enmeshed in the city's economic and social life. Local No. 226 held its regular Tuesday meetings at the Machinists' Hall, located at 126-1/2 Fourth Street. R. Roy Whitsett was recording secretary and Chester J. Vanderpool financial secretary.

Early in February 1920, William Hutcheson arrived in Portland in the course of the tour of western locals that had led to the return of No. 1020 to the carpenters' fold. That year, he presided over an organization of 350,000 members, making the carpenters' the most powerful craft union in the nation. In his Portland speech, he said that he was attempting to resolve jurisdictional disputes with various other West Coast unions, such as the maritime workers, the bridge and structural iron workers, and the pile drivers.[5] Assimilation by the United Brotherhood of Carpenters of locals in those fields whose members did carpenters' tasks would make the carpenters stronger, he noted. In that spirit, he played a significant role during his visit in bringing the caulkers as well as the shipwrights back into the carpenters' orbit.

In a speech to a joint assembly of all the Portland carpenters' locals on 3 February, Hutcheson praised a new and unusual arrangement devised by the Portland Building Trades Council to bring all the city's union carpenters up to the latest wage increases (negotiated during the summer of 1919). The Building Trades Council, with Bert Sleeman of No. 226 as the carpenters' delegate, had arranged with organized contractors to continue work on existing agreements at the old scale, with the stipulation that the council would assess itself for wage differentials and distribute the monies to the lower paid unionists, in order to give them parity with those on the new wage scale.[6] The enterprise was unique in the nation, but typical of the spirit of cooperation then emerging between labor and management in the Portland construction community.

This achievement was the more remarkable given that, in the wake of the current chauvinistic fervor and the AFL's well-publicized problems with government contractors over the open shop, employers' groups under the leadership of the National Association of Manufacturers had launched an offensive against the union movement. Advancing a program known as the "American Plan," which was merely the open shop by a more patriotic name, they hoped to cripple, if not destroy, organized labor by portraying the closed shop as unpatriotic.[7]

In the new decade, Local No. 226 continued to influence the city's labor community, largely through its energetic leadership. The men who emerged in the twenties constituted the third generation of activists to guide the local since its founding. Among the most prominent of the younger men was Sleeman, who, besides being the delegate to the Building Trades Council, was to hold many key offices in the city, in statewide labor and labor-management organization, and in government, sometimes contemporaneously. Dell Nickerson, who held dual membership in No. 226 and the painters' union, began serving his second term as president of the Central Labor Council while still in his teens.

These men, as well as the rank and file of No. 226, were driving forces in one of the major goals of Portland's labor unions. At its meeting of 24 February, the members of No. 226 bought two thousand dollars in stock (or 10 percent of the local's pledge) for the proposed Labor Temple building. The Labor Temple, a dream of the city's unionists since 1916, was conceived as a place to house all the city's unions. The war had delayed construction, but in November 1921 the building was completed. R.V. Hardwig, a member of No. 226, served on the committee of unionists overseeing construction.[8]

Early in the twenties also, the carpenters of No. 226 strengthened their local as well as the Portland construction industry by agreeing to participate in a vigorous apprenticeship program to train new, skilled craftsmen. The brotherhood had always had a training program, but it had never been particularly active in Oregon or Portland locals, apart from the modest program of the prewar years. It was not until 1966 that the United Brotherhood of Carpenters organized an apprenticeship department at its headquarters.

There had been no pressing need for such training before 1922 because U.S. immigration laws had permitted the entrance of large numbers of foreigners, among whom were skilled carpenters who had served rigorous apprenticeships in the Old World.[9] Most of them were immediately hired by large contractors and were often able to pass their knowledge on to their sons and favored co-workers in an informal way, thereby precluding the necessity for formal training programs. In 1921, however, in keeping with the country's isolationist outlook, the flow of immigrants was sharply reduced by the Immigration Restriction Act. When Congress subsequently passed the National Origins Act in 1924, immigration reduced to a trickle.

Portland's contractors, as well as local architects who had depended on the more gifted craftsmen for the proper execution of their designs, were distressed by the sudden curtailment of the stream of journeymen carpenters. They thus asked that No. 226 and the other unions of the Building Trades Council establish their own apprenticeship program, to ensure the entry of competent craftsmen into the building trades.

The unions embraced the proposal enthusiastically for reasons of their own. They recognized that a strong training program sponsored by the unions would guarantee them a high standard of workmanship which, in itself, was the key weapon against the open shop. The unions would thus be in a better position to bargain for improved working conditions and higher wages.

The old, and still growing, problem of good workmanship was a primary reason for the formation of the Portland Chapter of the Association for Building and Construction in January 1922. Local No. 226 was a charter member. The organization's function was to bring together all elements of the construction industry for the purposes of good fellowship and the achievement of mutually acceptable solutions to problems affecting the entire industry. At the early meetings of the Association, apprenticeship was the dominant topic of discussion.

At the meeting of 17 October 1922, the apprenticeship committee chairman, Dave L. Hoggan, a local contractor, commented on the need for training:

The apprenticeship problem virtually concerns everyone connected with the building industry. In fact, it reminds me of the farmer and his soil. He can take crops and crops out but, unless he enriches the soil, he soon realizes that he has a very inferior crop. So it is with the building industry. If we continue to get by with a little less quality, year after year, then ultimately we can expect to be in the same position as the farmer and his soured soil. We hear every day from the architect that the quality is not what it was of old in reference to labor. We hear from the mechanic . . . and . . . from the contractor as to quality and quantity, comparing present results with past. . . . I cannot believe that they intend to leave this most perplexing problem to drift with the tide and not leave any enriched working ground in which to perpetuate this most wonderful business of building."[10]

The apprenticeship program that evolved from this concern was modeled on a plan devised in 1923 by the New York branch of the American Building Congress, another national organization with which the Portland Chapter was affiliated. While the unions of the various trades in the curriculum determined the status of the journeyman, the Association for Building and Construction helped supervise the training. All segments of the industry contributed their expertise to the student's education. For example, a carpenter apprentice might be instructed by an architect, a contractor, and a materials dealer, as well as a journeyman carpenter, who imparted shop practice and theory. An apprentice attended vocational school for two-hour sessions on two evenings a week while working at his chosen trade during the day.[11] Wages for an apprentice were from $3.50 to $4.00 per day, depending on the trade.[12]

The key to the program's success in its early years was the guarantee to the student of a job on the student's completion of the course. This guarantee, in turn, was sustained by the building boom of the twenties. In November 1922, for instance, a speaker at an Association for Building and Construction dinner noted that Portland's building permits that year totaled $28 million.[13]

A steady stream of new mechanics entered the various building trades as a result of the training program instituted by the unions and the Association for Building and Construction. To take one example, in February 1927, when the first class had been completed, eight youths, including three who had trained as carpenters, emerged as journeymen from the graduation ceremony at Stevens School. The three carpenters were Lars Haugen, Adolphe Sandstrom, and David Steele.[14]

The final measure of the program's success is indicated by the fact that in 1927 a quota had to be imposed on the graduates' employment, to prevent individual contractors from monopolizing on those in a given class by hiring them before anyone else could. When a contractor attempted to defy the quota, he found himself beset by angry competitors.[15]

The cooperation between labor and management, reflected in the formation of the Association for Building and Construction, was aided by the general prosperity of the twenties, especially the sustained boom in construction throughout the United States. The decade of rapid urbanization and industrialization created a great demand for new housing, commercial and industrial buildings, and other structures. In December 1925, the Oregon state labor commissioner announced a figure of $40 million for all construction in the year. He expected the same pace for 1926 and was highly optimistic about the employment prospects for the state's construction-related labor force.[16]

With work abundant and the long-range forecast good, both labor and management could afford to be cordial in their mutual relationship.

Indeed, the familiarity of the working arrangements between Portland's carpenters and their employers fostered an unofficial quota system for work on construction sites. As an example, when a journeyman fitted and hung hardwood doors, he could go home whenever the work was completed, even if he had put in only six and a half or seven hours. (Not that such a task was especially easy. Doors came in random sizes, half an inch to three-quarters of an inch oversize, with side stiles of random length and width. All four sides had to be ripped to length with handsaws and trued with hand planes. That was also true of jambs. There were no power tools at jobsites.)[17]

Even contract negotiations for the carpenters and the other building trades were somewhat free from trouble in Portland. The building trades began to negotiate as a group through the Building Trades Council with contractors represented by the Associated General Contractors (the construction employers' association) in 1924.[18] Before that, each trade had bargained separately with the individual contractors, an arrangement complicated by the fact that each trade was responsible for wage negotiations for its helpers. Laborers traditionally got less than half what journeymen made, so that when carpenters were getting $1.00 per hour, laborers received $.40.

For some time this cooperation was pleasant for both sides, minimizing both competitive rancor in favor of the prestige gained by higher wage settlements on the union's part and strategies of divide-and-conquer by the employers. The unions thus achieved a relative parity in hours and wages. A few locals had previously got ahead of No. 226 in hours and had already reached the labor movement's goal—the forty-hour week. The carpenters, on the other hand, worked forty-five hours (five eight-hour days and five hours on Saturday). At 1:00 P.M. on Saturdays, they were paid and given the rest of the day off. Some trades still worked forty-eight-hour weeks, or six eight-hour days.[19]

Prosperity and tranquillity in Portland's construction labor unions prevailed for most of the twenties. However, developments in labor economics were beginning to work to the detriment of the construction trades, particularly the carpenters. For one thing, in 1926, a $1.00-per-day wage hike put an extra $5.50 a week in carpenters' pay envelopes until, in

1928, the contract expired under which the raise was granted. The raise touched off nationwide concern among construction employers that wages were getting out of hand. Many contractors began to resist the idea of future increases and to question the unions' position that workers' real wages should rise in response to increases in productivity.[20] A spokesman for the New York Building Trades Employers Association argued that the new construction boom actually masked a decline in productivity catalyzed by the social trends of the decade: "With the vast amount of building throughout the country and restriction of immigration, there has been . . . a condition where the . . . careless worker is employed almost on parity with the good workman, with the result that the production of the good workman has been reduced."[21] Employers resolved to adhere to the yardstick of supply and demand among the work force in reviewing the merits of further pay raises. (Portland carpenters with long memories might have recalled the issues of the strike of 1903.)

From the carpenter union's vantage, at least locally, this was a significant attitude. The union's bargaining position was still being weakened by the continued existence of the open shop and by the "camp follower," as the *Labor Press* labeled the unorganized workman—generally an older man who had never belonged to the union. He earned perhaps fifty cents less per hour than the union carpenter, probably felt comfortable with his wage, and believed the union couldn't do much for him. Yet when union scale was raised, he got a raise. "Even those who refuse to share the benefits," said the *Labor Press*, "cannot escape the benefits."[22]

A more insidious—if related—development for the carpenters and other Portland construction unions occurred in 1925. Like the persistence of the so-called camp follower, it directly and adversely affected the ability of the organized skilled craftsmen, such as the carpenters, to negotiate.

In 1925, construction helpers of all trades organized themselves under the Building Laborers' Union. This much-strengthened union was quickly able to establish a uniform pay scale for its members of sixty cents per hour. The Building Laborers also joined the Portland Building Trades Council and negotiated contracts with the Associated General Contractors as part of the single body that characterized the council throughout the 1920s, 1930s, and 1940s. Contracts resulting from this alliance generally maintained a forty-cent differential between skilled craftsmen and laborers, in addition to double time for overtime by skilled workmen, as opposed to time and a half for laborers. Nevertheless, the Building Laborers were able to negotiate premium wage rates for such specialized jobs as those of the jackhammer operator, creosoter, and high-scaffolding worker. During construction booms such as that of the twenties, as many as half the Building Laborers were thus able to take home wages equal to or greater than those of the journeyman carpenters.[23]

This development undermined the carpenters' morale. A carpenter and his helper might take home virtually the same pay, but it was necessary for the former also to buy and maintain his own tools, at a cost of between five hundred and one thousand dollars. A laborer furnished nothing except a pair of gloves and a rule. He had no particular responsibility save his own industriousness. Carpenters were also expected to supervise laborers and could be held responsible for their work.[24]

Many Portland carpenters felt themselves undercompensated when compared with building laborers. Some of the more disgruntled actually left the craft and became laborers. Some laborers who might otherwise have aspired to be journeyman carpenters never entered the more skilled trade, preferring the less demanding occupation of labor.[25]

The cumulative effect of the formation of the Building Laborers, however, was of far greater significance to the carpenters' locals than any retardation or diversion of individual ambitions. For in time this development, coupled with the restrictions on immigration, more than offset the numbers entering apprenticeship from other avenues. The outcome was to make more room for the unschooled type of craftsman, the "camp follower," and to defeat, or at least weaken, the reasons for the apprenticeship program. When that occurred, the bargaining position of organized carpenters was undermined against the supply-and-demand position of employers.

The decade also saw the craft of carpentry move further and further into the machine age, particularly in the Pacific Northwest. It was a development that cut two ways. Skilled hand carpenters, who normally kept themselves busy during the dismal winters making doors, sashes, and other cabinetry products, found themselves in about mid-decade faced with competition from factories that produced such things in quantity. This was an outcome of the highly effective campaign of the Pacific Coast Lumbermen's Association to gain acceptance of the indigenous Douglas fir as a cheap, attractive, and abundant wood for use in all kinds of construction projects.[26] Enthusiastic Northwest entrepreneurs, recognizing the truth of this assertion, as well as the market created by the building boom, began to set up door factories. Tacoma soon became the door capital of the world, with ten or twelve factories working full time. The Wheeler & Osgood plant was reputed to turn out thirty thousand doors a day at its peak.[27] Several factories in Portland also competed well. Nicolai Door, M & M Woodworking, Central Door, and Nicolai Sash & Door were the most prominent. Nicolai made some five thousand doors a day in 1923.

The hand carpenters, perhaps confident of the long-term nature of the increase in construction, made no real effort to compete with the door factories. At about the same time, carpenters allowed other workers to take over roofing and laying floors. The result was a singular loss of work and hours that soon became permanent.[28]

Another encroachment was made on the carpenters when the electric table saw appeared at the worksite in approximately 1928.[29] This device cut hours as well as wood, but also raised productivity.

The mass production of doors, windows, and sashes was transformed into a benefit for the United Brotherhood of Carpenters by two members of Local No. 583. George Ankeny and Jess Stout were instrumental in bringing the millmen (also known as "sawdust savages") of the door factories into the United Brotherhood of Carpenters.[30] The doormakers were put into Local No. 1120. The first union-label door in the United States came out of the M & M factory of Charlie and Jim Malarkey in 1927.

Local No. 1020 had been suspended from the United Brotherhood of Carpenters in September 1919. On 10 March 1920, it was rechartered by General President Hutcheson. In the period after the war and throughout the twenties, several other locals were granted charters by the union. Their diversity indicates the brotherhood's adaptability to the changing nature of work in the rapid technological advance. Local No. 2218, a general-construction organization, with activities in the shipyards, came into being on 11 July 1919. It consolidated with No. 1020 in 1971. Local No. 2416, a pile-driver and dock and wharf builders' group, was chartered on 17 March 1920. A lathers' local, No. 2154, was chartered on 31 March 1924.

SEVEN
Depression and War, 1930-1945

THE UNITED STATES PREPARED FOR THE decade of the 1930s with a buoyant sense of confidence.

The country seemed to be capably led by the business-oriented Republican party and President Herbert Hoover, a brilliant mining engineer, statesman, and self-made millionaire. The nationwide prosperity that had been nurtured by Harding and Coolidge from the end of the war throughout the bustling 1920s appeared destined to last forever.

On the other hand, a few scattered but ominous signs of economic difficulty ahead became apparent as early as the summer of 1928, when construction slowed dramatically in parts of the East and Midwest. In August 1929 the *Carpenter* magazine noted this and warned, "We as a nation are facing a situation that is phenomenal, in that while we have abundant resources, a vast accumulation of capital and equipment, and large numbers of highly skilled workers capable of more production than at any time in the history of civilization, yet millions of workers do not have an opportunity for regular and steady work." The portents, however, came either too early or too late for a government and a people blinded by ease and optimism and for an economy suffering from hidden but chronic and fundamental dislocations.

By 1929, American banking, private business, and personal fortunes were tied together in a largely unregulated financial system marked by pyramided investments, margin-stock buying, and overloaned banks. This precarious situation was complicated by the collapse of the international trading system, occasioned by the ferocious international protectionism that had prevailed since the Great War. High tariffs and the return of European battlefields to peacetime cultivation kept American farm produce out of Europe. American agricultural workers, thus thrown out of work, migrated to the cities, where they found themselves unemployed.

The collapse of the financial markets after the crash of 24 October 1929 instigated an eventual paralysis of the American economy. Considering the enormity and scope of the collapse, there was little anyone could do to return the nation to prosperity quickly.

In May 1930, Hoover announced, "We have now passed the worst and . . . shall rapidly recover." Others reached a different conclusion. In 1929, new capital issues—a good indicator of the level of investment—had reached $10 billion. In 1930, the figure was $7 billion. By 1932, it was $1 billion. In 1929, corporate profits were at $8.4 billion; in 1932, $3.4 billion. In 1929, 659 banks collapsed. Depositors lost about $200 million. In 1931, 2,294 banks with deposits of almost $1.7 billion were lost. From 1929 to 1932, over one hundred thousand businesses failed. By mid-1932, industrial production was off 51 percent from the level of 1929. Four million people found themselves unemployed in October 1930. Americans without jobs totaled eleven million in 1932. Even those who kept their jobs in factories and farms were hurt by the ever-growing disaster as wages and hours were cut. By 1932, the national income had deteriorated to $49 billion from a figure of $81 billion in 1929, as average wages fell some 60 percent and average salaries 40 percent.

The nation's economic problems were felt before the Great Crash of 1929 in the state of Oregon. A softening of demand for wood products resulted from the construction slump of the late twenties and caught Oregon's mills with large inventories and no buyers. The state's other leading industry, agriculture, was also crippled by low demand. After the crash, Oregon's economy followed the spectacular decline of the nation's. In 1930, sales volume in the state declined 20 percent. A year later, business was off another 23 percent. In 1932, 866 Oregon manufacturing plants went out of business; employment declined to 48 percent in the timber industry. Twenty percent of the work force in Portland was laid off. This statistic translated into twenty-four thousand unemployed persons.

Hoover's plans to combat the Depression were modest. He believed the economy was basically sound and that the natural forces of the free market would eventually correct the nation's problems. Consequently, he initially offered only cuts in personal and corporate taxes to encourage investment and a meager public-works program to stimulate construction. Though these measures were quite inadequate to effect a recovery in 1930, the president clung stubbornly to his position. The Democratic minority fashioned an unemployment-relief bill in the lame-duck session of Congress that year, but he remained convinced that the government should stay out of private business and that relief was best left to local government and private charities. He gave freely of his concern and encouragement, but stingily of the resources of the federal government.

In Portland, the signs of hard times were evident all over the city. Perhaps the most prominent was "Hooverville," a shantytown of dispossessed and indigent people, which sprang up in Sullivan's Gulch on the city's east side, between Northeast Grand and Twenty-first avenues. Unemployed workers and boarded-up businesses were omnipresent, reminding Portlanders of the nation's monumental difficulties. The city's public and private leadership, in the absence of strong action from Washington, D.C., addressed itself to the task of righting the situation locally.

Among the most vigorous respondents to the crisis was Portland's community of organized labor. The carpenters' union was at the forefront of activities to succor the needy and promote recovery. In December 1929, with their own resources restricted, the members of No. 226 donated $15 toward Christmas presents for needy children. In February 1930, the ubiquitous Bert Sleeman of No. 226 represented the carpenters in a meeting convened at the Multnomah Hotel by Governor Albin W. Norblad to enlist cooperation from all sectors of the economy for Hoover's program to fight the Depression. Many labor, financial, industrial, and political leaders attended. Little of substance came from the conference, but all present pledged cooperation and gave evidence of concern and a disposition toward common action.

As the year wore on and the situation worsened, local labor began to formulate its own prescription for recovery in the city. Union spokesmen urged an offensive against inertia through a public-works program. A survey of local taxation published by the *Labor Press* in early April indicated that Portland's tax rate was one of the nation's lowest, at $1.71 per capita, as against Atlanta's, the highest at $2.46. The paper pointed out that a judicious program of public-works projects, such as the proposed (and much needed) Fremont Bridge, would add little to the local tax burden, but would alleviate unemployment in the construction industry to a great degree.

Representatives of the Central Labor Council, the Building Trades Council, the carpenters, local contractors, and the *Labor Press* lobbied furiously for the Fremont Bridge, but when it came before the voters in May 1930 in a $6.5 million bond measure, they rejected it. Ironically, the St. Johns Bridge, endorsed by the electorate during the prosperous year of 1928, was to be completed in June 1931 on schedule and under budget, a much-needed boost to civic morale. It may have symbolized a missed opportunity, as no new Willamette River bridges were authorized until 1959, when the Morrison Bridge was replaced. The Fremont Bridge was not built until 1970.

The *Labor Press* expanded on its blueprint for recovery in a front-page editorial of its issue of 29 June 1930. Aptly entitled "Just a Dream," the essay asked: "Why should not America do a good thing today . . . ? Why not create good homes by the millions, raise the whole national living standard and end unemployment?"[1] If this solution to the economic woes warmed the hearts of the carpenters, the reason it was unworkable was nonetheless clear. In Portland (as in other cities and towns throughout the United States), the banks were insolvent. Capital and eligible borrowers were not available. In the spring of 1931, the U.S. National Bank of Oregon had only a quarter of its deposits in the hands of Portland borrowers. By the end of the year, the Hibernia Commercial and Savings Bank, the city's sixth largest financial institution, chronically short of liquid assets that year, closed its doors.

By mid-June 1931, the unemployment rate in Portland had declined somewhat, to 17,655. At the same time, building permits totaling almost five hundred thousand dollars worth of new construction were entered at City Hall. The carpenters and the rest of the building trades, however, remained the most distressed of Portland's unions, with a majority of their members idled.

Throughout the Depression, the Labor Temple at Southwest Fourth and Jefferson was a focus of activity and an anchor of hope for men cut loose from their jobs. Most of the larger unions had offices there, and the unemployed of the various trades usually packed the place, commiserating, milling round, and sipping coffee. Carpenters and other construction workers had another motive for their daily visits. Whenever a truck from the Jones Lumber Company next door set out with a load of materials, the union men would follow it to the jobsite, hoping to find work there.[2] Meanwhile, the carpenters' leadership remained active in state labor affairs. In July 1931, for example, David Duff, Bert Sleeman, and Charles Kolb of No. 226 attended the convention of the State Council of Carpenters in Salem. At the same time, the Portland Building Trades Council acted to save and to generate as many jobs in the construction industry as possible. First, the unions notified the Associated General Contractors that their members would accept a six-hour day, but warned that they would not take wage cuts. Second, they appointed a committee to monitor the progress of prospective public-works projects, making sure that politicians who might be called upon to vote them up or down were properly educated as to their benefits, costs, and timing; that officials received all relevant documents; that contracts were signed in a timely fashion; and so forth.

In October 1931, this strategy was tested when Ralph Clyde, a city councilman, attempted to stall the construction of the public market at the foot of Southwest Yamhill Street on the Willamette River in downtown. The project, which had attracted the capital of many of the city's leading businessmen, including John C. Ainsworth of the U.S. National Bank,

Julius Meier of the Meier and Frank Department Store, and Philip Jackson, former publisher of the *Oregon Journal*, was to cost about $1.5 million. Despite such backing, the market was questionable in a number of respects, which Clyde aired publicly. It seemed to consumers and merchants to be too far from the center of the downtown shopping area; though ostensibly a public project, it would in reality be a private venture that had been pressed on the city by influential investors; the presence of a commercial building along the waterfront appeared to violate the accepted vision of the city's planners since the turn of the century.

The whole issue caused a major brouhaha, with fiery editorials from newspapers on both sides of the argument, petitions, revelations of bribery, public hearings, and legal actions. The argument that eventually carried the most weight was the one advanced by the *Labor Press*, the Building Trades, and the Civic Emergency Committee, a group of prominent citizens appointed to plan the city's recovery. They all insisted that the Front Street Market, as it came to be called, represented a significant contribution to unemployment relief and noted that construction could begin soon after approval. A loan of $775,000 from the Reconstruction Finance Corporation, an institution created by the Hoover administration to stimulate capital formation, was negotiated in the fall of 1932 to subsidize construction.[3] To some extent, the loan appeased some of the project's opponents, and the city council then endorsed its construction.

Ground was broken for the market in June 1933. It was completed before Christmas. Commissioner Clyde had predicted that the Front Street Market would be a white elephant, and he was right. Never fully occupied, by the beginning of 1936 it was in serious financial difficulty. In 1946, the *Oregon Journal* purchased the building, which was later razed to make way for a park. If the Front Street Market served any real purpose, it was to employ more than two hundred men and to spend over $500,000 on building it at a time when almost no construction was occurring in Portland. In that instance, at least, the public-works lobbying group of the Building Trades Council served its purpose. Later municipal projects championed by the construction unions—widening streets, building railroad trestles—were turned down by the city council for lack of funds.

The carpenters and the other Building Trades unions were still trying to solve the city's unemployment in the spring of 1932 when they joined local groups, such as the Unemployed Citizens League, in promoting a scrip issue that would subsidize public-works employment on much-needed city projects. Workers on public projects could use the scrip—in essence, temporary currency—as payment for the goods of cooperating merchants. The merchants could redeem the scrip at the county treasurer's office. Revenues to subsidize the scrip would come from the sale of stamps authorized by the county. An advisory board, with Dell Nickerson of No. 226 as a member, was formed. When the sale of employment-relief bonds fell short of the expected figure in the winter of 1933, the scrip plan was put into effect through joint city-county action, with an initial issue of $30,000. Great skepticism was expressed by many members of the business community, including the owners of Meier and Frank and local bankers. Active opposition came from some prominent conservatives like Leslie Scott, state highway commission chairman and part owner of the *Oregonian*.[4]

Some eighteen thousand people signed up for jobs in the public-works projects to be subsidized by the scrip after its approval in March 1933. Among the projects on which many of them were employed was the remodeling and redecorating of Portland's City Hall.[5]

The election of Franklin Roosevelt in November 1932, and the hundred-day flurry of legislation that followed his inauguration in March 1933, were tonics to a nation buffeted by fortune for two years. But the advent of Roosevelt's New Deal, as it became known, was only the end of the beginning of the Depression, not the beginning of the end.

Among the few local private construction projects of 1933 was the remodeling of the Weinhard Brewery at Southwest Twelfth and Burnside. The $300,000 project was undertaken by Hoffman Construction Company, using union carpenters. However, this positive note in Portland's construction industry was temporarily negated by some minor flooding at the seawall site of the Front Street Market during late June. The high water temporarily threw two five-hour shifts from the building trades unions out of work.

The meagerness of privately financed new construction in Portland in 1933 kept the building industry's attention focused on the New Deal legislation. It was a frequently voiced hope by those connected with construction work that the new laws would provide financing for, or otherwise stimulate, building activity. In July, architects, contractors, construction-materials dealers, the Building Trades Council, and the Oregon Building Congress, encouraged by the vigor of the new administration, created a committee to monitor the allocation of federal funds and to ensure that a significant amount of the monies sent to Oregon was earmarked for new construction. The carpenters' interests were represented by Dell Nickerson, president of No. 226, who sat on the committee as the voice of the Building Trades Council.[6]

The most promising piece of legislation, so far as the construction industry was concerned, appeared to be the National Industrial Recovery Act of 16 June 1933. The act provided a public-works appropriation of more than $3 billion; moreover, Section 7(a) of the act held out a great deal of hope for unions. It stated "employees shall have the right to organize and bargain collectively through representatives of their own choosing," and that "employers shall comply with the maximum hours of labor, minimum rates of pay, and other conditions of employment, approved or prescribed by the President." It threw the weight of the federal government and the prestige of the presidency behind organized labor.[7] Coming at a time when West Coast unionism was at one of the lowest ebbs in its existence, the government's statutory endorsement could only be described as a shot in the arm. The act was later invalidated by the u.s. Supreme Court, but the principle of organized labor's legitimacy was intrinsic to the National Labor Relations Act of 5 July 1935. This act, also known as the Wagner Act, proved to be the legal foundation for collective bargaining upon which labor was able to build an aggressive organizing campaign in the post-Depression era.

While the carpenters and others waited for the fruits of the National Industrial Recovery Act to ripen, the autumn of 1933 brought a harvest of federal dollars and nourishment for the construction industry from another source. Since 1913, it had been the dream of business and political leaders throughout the Northwest to harness the wild waters of the Columbia River for irrigation, reclamation, flood control, and the generation of cheap hydroelectric power. Since his 1932 campaign, Roosevelt had been on record as favoring a series of dams on the river for such purposes. After much lobbying by Senator Charles McNary and Representative Charles Martin of Oregon, he committed $31 million in federal funds to the construction of a dam at Warrendale, some thirty-five miles east of Portland, to be known as Bonneville. The dam, a "concrete gravity ogee-crust gate-controlled structure," was begun in the spring of 1934 with nearly $20.25 million of Works Progress Administration (WPA) funds.[8]

The dam, which required hundreds of pile drivers to pour the foundations and carpenters to build scaffolding and cement forms, was a godsend to Portland's carpenters. For the initial phases of construction, the contractors were Columbia Construction and Guy F. Atkinson, Inc. Men were hired at the U.S. employment office about a block from the Labor Temple, where Sleeman was headquartered.

As district council business agent, Sleeman had an informal arrangement with the government employment agents. He sent union members through the hall for assignments at the dam, rather than soliciting the work himself, thus allowing the employment agents to take credit for the new hirings. The agents, for their part, agreed to send nonunion hires to Sleeman at the Labor Temple so that they could be unionized.[9] This worked well for all concerned, particularly No. 226, which was at the Labor Temple. Local No. 583, however, out in North Portland, resented the fact that the new hires flocked to No. 226 while it remained relatively small and weak.[10] However, since the object of the arrangement—to provide jobs to union carpenters in the most expedient manner and to make sure that nonunion carpenters who got work at the dam were quickly enrolled in the union—was of primary importance, the tension between the two locals was minimal.

Nevertheless, the Depression caused internal divisions in the American labor movement, involving the carpenters in debilitating interactive warfare from the mid-thirties to the mid-fifties. These divisions resulted from the rise of the Congress of Industrial Organizations (CIO), a vehicle for industrial unionism formed after the walkout by John L. Lewis, the legendary leader of the United Mineworkers, from the AFL convention of 1935.[11] Lewis and his allies believed that unions structured along industrial rather than craft lines would provide more effective representation for the millions of mass-production workers, whose collective-bargaining position differed greatly from that of the skilled craftsmen of the old and conservative business unions of the AFL, like the carpenters'.[12] Over the years, the carpenters (and other craft unions) had expanded to encompass mass-production workers such as the millmen of box factories and planing mills, but although these workers were in the United Brotherhood of Carpenters, their wages remained lower than those of construction carpenters. Nor did they receive full financial benefits.[13] Passions were so inflamed over industrial unionism that Lewis and Hutcheson of the carpenters came to blows on the floor of the convention.

Across the nation there began a long and rancorous struggle between the AFL and the CIO for collective-bargaining rights in industries previously organized by the AFL. In Oregon, besides the maritime trades, a particular theater of conflict was the lumber industry. The carpenters became embroiled from the outset because of their slowly growing interest in the lumber industry.

The large numbers of wood-products workers (perhaps one hundred thousand in the mid-thirties) made the carpenters' interest natural. Yet the organizing task was too much for the union's leadership to contemplate in the Depression years, especially in an industrial setting. But when the AFL's effort in the logging camps and sawmills of the Northwest showed results, the United Brotherhood of Carpenters began to appreciate the opportunity looming before it. By August 1934, it was claiming jurisdiction over all branches of the industry, from logging to finishing mills.

By 1935, the carpenters had gained control over the new locals created by AFL organizers. These, however, were not necessarily happy with the transfer. The most disaffected among them struck, paralyzing the Northwest wood-products industry.

Abe Muir, a member of the general executive board of the United Brotherhood of Carpenters and an industry activist, eventually negotiated an agreement that kept the locals within the brotherhood. Nonetheless, the most recalcitrant locals continued to resist through an ad hoc council. Muir responded by revoking their charters, one of which was that of Millman's Local No. 2658 of Portland. He replaced the dissidents with United Brotherhood of Carpenters loyalists, and the energy of the strike flagged. Men went back to work in an atmosphere of superficial calm, but the industry was polarized.

The United Brotherhood of Carpenters announced that it had organized seventy thousand workers in two hundred locals by the end of the strike in 1936. But in September of that year, the carpenters' opponents formed the Federation of Woodworkers, an organization strongly in sympathy with the CIO. Harold Pritchett, a Canadian of well-established Communist sympathies, was elected president. The Federation of Woodworkers sent delegates to the United Brotherhood of Carpenters convention in Lakeland, Florida, in December 1936. They were a mixed bag of Communists, CIO advocates and pro-United Brotherhood of Carpenters activists.

At the convention, the federation delegates requested a vote in the proceedings, citing the past contributions of their locals in per-capita taxes to the United Brotherhood of Carpenters' treasury as a symbol of their rights. The staid carpenters, reflecting on the presence in their midst of Communists, CIO sympathizers, and even—among loggers—old-time Wobblies, found the prospect of such influence too much to contemplate. They rejected the federationists' credentials.[14]

The lumber workers returned from the convention by way of Washington, D.C., where they consulted inconclusively with Lewis. The CIO, meanwhile, was enjoying mounting success in organizing the wood-products industry in the Pacific Northwest. Despite the fact that a major faction of the Federation of Woodworkers wished to remain with the carpenters, the momentum of events was carrying it toward industrial unionism. In July 1937, the federation members turned overwhelmingly to the CIO as the result of a referendum on the issue. The International Woodworkers of America emerged as their bargaining agent.

The United Brotherhood of Carpenters had been maladroit in handling the federation. Its leadership had virtually assured that the CIO would be strengthened by one hundred thousand members. Now they would pay in their own shops. One example of the consequences of this polarization occurred in Portland, in a finishing mill—a segment of the industry previously thought to be an inviolate enclave of United Brotherhood of Carpenters unionism.

The Plylock Company, in the St. Johns district, was reputed to be the first plywood manufacturing facility in the world. When Plylock was organized by the CIO, the millmen of the United Brotherhood of Carpenters' Local No. 1746 refused to use Plylock plywood in the manufacture of doors at the M & M plant, where most of the members worked. Tom Malarkey, owner of both Plylock and M & M, thereupon sued the CIO in order to break the boycott, arguing that the Plylock workers had broken their AFL contract before it expired. He won.[15] Ironically, the Plylock contract was regarded as a model for the industry, by which other agreements could be judged in all respects. Sleeman, for example, had a succinct negotiating posture for plywood mills: "Malarkey [Plylock] or better."[16]

The warfare between the AFL and the CIO continued through the forties and fifties, ending only with the merger of the two groups in 1955.[17] In the meantime, the carpenters lost many of the forest-products workers, especially those in the sawmills, to the International Woodworkers of America.

As the Depression wore on, the battle for prosperity in Portland waxed and waned, but in the construction industry, adversity had one happy by-product. Labor and management drew closer together, as it became increasingly clear to both the Building Trades Council and the Associated General Contractors that the efforts of the New Dealers could go only so far toward the resurrection of an economy in which construction might thrive.

Thus, in the spring of 1936, when the Building Trades Council and the Associated General Contractors undertook contract negotiations, they wove into their deliberations plans for a future construction market that would serve investors and consumers by holding down costs. A joint statement issued on the completion of negotiations by Bronsel R. Mathis of the council and James M. Scudder of the contractors said:

> [B]oth parties have realized the importance of doing everything
> possible to stimulate private construction in order to provide employment when the present government-sponsored building activity
> slows up. It is hoped that our agreement to hold labor costs on
> construction at their present levels will be conducive to a substantial

increase in private construction in the Portland area during this
year.

Translated into total construction costs, the rise in wages to go into
effect on 1 January 1937 would mean an additional 5 percent increase on the
total cost of a building.[18]

There was reason to be concerned. The recovery of the economy in
Roosevelt's second term was fragile and slow to evolve. Although it was
occurring (led by residential building, which was benefiting from lower
labor costs and easier money), eight million people were unemployed
nationally, and by autumn the cost of living had risen 16 percent from the
same period in 1933.[19]

One year later, this basic weakness took its toll as construction began
to lag nationwide. The lull affected Oregon, but a promise of relief was
afforded by movement in municipal public works. For one thing, the
Portland City Council began to consider rebuilding the Morrison Street
Bridge. Naturally, the carpenters and the Building Trades Council lobbied
ardently for the project. But the bridge was not rebuilt until 1955, and a
municipal natatorium, also on the drawing boards, never reached the
groundbreaking stage. Similarly, plans for a municipal housing authority
were bruited about by civic leaders, encouraged by the Building Trades
Council, but it was only in 1941, with the influx of shipyard workers to the
city as industry prepared for war, that the Housing Authority of Portland
was created, with an accompanying increase in the construction of low-
cost housing.[20]

In 1939, however, Portland's economy continued in its erratic course
so far as construction was concerned. In the spring, it improved again and
the Building Trades, eager to seize the initiative, organized a housing
show. It opened in early June and created several jobs. As summer advanced, however, building slowed again. By the end of the year, there was
little activity, yet the first ten months of the year showed an improvement
over the same period in 1938, with 4,129 building permits issued in 1939, for
a total of $7.1 million in construction, against 3,894 permits, totaling $5.6
million in 1938.[21]

By 1940, there was confidence among Portland's labor leaders that the economy was on the move again. A *Labor Press* survey revealed that most of them viewed the new year as possibly the best for a decade.[22] Dell Nickerson, by that time secretary-treasurer of the Oregon State Federation of Labor, stated the perennial Oregon sentiment about economic development: "I give it as my opinion that the best fortune which could come to Portland in 1940 would be an increase in jobs through establishment of new industries and expansion of those now here, but without an increase of population."[23]

Mathis of the Building Trades Council meanwhile touted 1940 as the best year ever for members of the public to build houses. Listing five reasons to build immediately, he added a sixth that characterized the construction unions after the Depression: "Labor is cheaper, better, and more plentiful. There is no labor trouble in the building trades."[24]

The generally busy pace of construction included the Heathman Hotel project on Southwest Broadway in downtown Portland. The Building Trades Council's protest against the construction of a new armory by WPA labor was also a sign of the passing of hard times and with it the relevance of the New Deal measures once regarded as essential to collective and individual economic survival.[25] To the unions, the WPA was like the green-hand labor of the late nineteenth century—cheap, unorganized, and unfairly competitive with union craftsmen. This was especially so in 1940, when, after the proliferation of public works during the thirties, it became virtually impossible to make or enforce the kind of agreement Sleeman had arranged with the WPA on the Bonneville Dam.

"We Repeat: America Keep Out," the *Labor Press* headlined its lead editorial of 22 September 1939.[26] Germany had invaded Poland on 1 September, touching off World War II. In the false calm of the "phony" war that ensued, many voices were raised, as they had been in World War I, against American intervention in the European conflict. Organized labor's was again among them. Neutrality was the byword, the *Labor Press* asserted, from top to bottom in the ranks of the union movement—from President William Green of the AFL and the officers of the Oregon State Federation of Labor to the editors of the newspaper and the rank and file.[27]

It was, nevertheless, a short leap in time, if not sentiment, to the screaming headline of 12 December 1941: "AFL Backs War."[28] Fred

Manash, secretary of the Building Trades Council, spoke for the construction trades on that date, five days after Pearl Harbor, when he told the paper:

> I subscribe 100% to the statements of President Roosevelt in that we must see to it that the treacherous governments of Japan, Italy, and Germany must be wiped off the earth and union labor shall do its part in accomplishing ultimate victory over its enemies.[29]

The pressure had been mounting for America's involvement in the confrontation with fascism since the late thirties. The Allies had been clamoring for it, and Roosevelt had been preparing the ground for some years with devices such as the "Quarantine of Aggressors" speech of 1937 and the lend-lease program of aid to Great Britain initiated in 1941. Japan's attack on the U.S. Pacific fleet of 7 December was simply the last piece of a tragic puzzle.

In Portland, despite the *Labor Press* editorial of 1939, events seemed to be pushing the city's economy, not to mention its collective psyche, toward a war footing. In 1940 defense or quasi-defense projects, such as the armory and the new airport by the Columbia River, dominated the construction scene. (Like the armory, the airport concerned the unions because of the contractor's reliance on WPA labor.)[30] In August 1941, the Building Trades Department of the AFL signed a no-strike agreement with the federal government on a U.S. defense construction project.[31] On Labor Day, Nickerson, speaking for the Oregon State Federation of Labor, said that Oregon labor was ready for a national emergency. The federation would renounce the stoppage of work in defense industries. He could not, he said, exaggerate the importance of such work.[32] In the carpenters' union halls and in union halls across the city, each meeting began with the Pledge of Allegiance.[33] Patriotism was in the air. An economic boom was in the wind.

In fact, the war in Europe ended the Depression for Americans.[34] Even before the United States' entry, war-related industries began to prepare as the country became, in Roosevelt's phrase, "the arsenal of democracy." In January 1941, Henry Kaiser brought to Portland a contract let by the British government for the construction of thirty-one cargo ships.[35] At a site he acquired on the banks of the Willamette near the St. Johns district of North Portland, he prepared to build an eight-way yard. By 19 May 1941, the yard's first Liberty ship, the *Star of Oregon*, slid down the ways and put to sea. By mid-1942, Kaiser had opened a yard in Vancouver to produce 50 baby aircraft escort carriers and another at Swan Island in the Willamette for the production of 147 T-2 tankers. With 31 ways in production, Portland was the national leader in Liberty and Victory ship construction.[36]

Kaiser's Portland-area yards became the phenomenon of wartime shipbuilding under the u.s. Maritime Commission. By December 1942, Kaiser's firm, Oregon Shipbuilding Company, had reduced construction time on a Liberty ship, from keel-laying to delivery, from 226 days to an average of just over 33 days.[37] In an astounding feat, Oregon Ship delivered one vessel in 10 days. By the end of 1942, West Coast shipyards had delivered 60 percent of the nation's Liberty ships. Oregon Ship delivered one-third of the West Coast total, or one-fifth of the nation's vessels, more than doubling the total for which it had originally contracted.[38] By the end of the war, Kaiser's Portland-area yards had delivered 455.

Among the reasons for this efficiency, perhaps foremost was the fact that Kaiser was an innovator, unafraid to try new methods. In this respect, his intensive application of a large labor force employing mass-production techniques was crucial.[39] The routine use of critical path planning—forecasting bottlenecks in production through scientific studies—was another new method that speeded the manufacturing process in the Portland yards.[40]

Also significant was the availability in the Portland area of talented shipwrights from World War 1 and Kaiser's own dam builders from the Grand Coulee and Bonneville projects. From the outset, platoons of workers from across the country, unfamiliar with the marine crafts, either were recruited by Kaiser or simply showed up in his employment offices in Portland. With government-developed training programs, they were put to work in short order. But it was the fund of knowledge of the shipwrights and the dam builders that made the Kaiser yards hum.

The shipwrights and carpenters on the dam projects held the keys to the entire shipbuilding enterprise. Other crafts were far more numerous in the yards—at Oregon Ship, the greatest craft percentage was of welders, with an average of 22.25 percent for all vessel types, compared with just over 4.5 percent of shipwrights—but the shipwrights were alone in having been trained to work in three dimensions (the other crafts worked only in two), and specifically in cones, which is how ships are laid out.[41] This was crucial to understanding a ship's overall construction, which had to be square to within one-eighth of an inch.[42]

Those carpenters with experience on the dams shared Kaiser's openness to improvisation. They had learned to overcome new obstacles on the huge dams through imagination, native intelligence, and trial and error; now, in the midst of the national emergency, they attacked shipbuilding in the same way. As foremen and supervisors, their spirit spread to the young workers under them who were eager to increase their efficiency and contribute to the war effort.

Generally, the shipyard carpenters built scaffolding, shoring, cabinets, woodfittings for interiors, and furniture. In the mold loft, they built repetitive patterns like ships' ribs.[44] But this list does not altogether convey a sense of the carpenters' responsibilities in the yards, where they were involved in construction from the keel laying to the christening.[45]

All the crafts found working conditions in the Kaiser yards generally favorable. In his early years in the construction business, Henry Kaiser had resisted unionization. After early experimentation with the open shop on projects such as Boulder Dam, however, he tried the union shop at Grand Coulee, where costs per yard of concrete proved to be lower than at Boulder. From then on, the Kaiser management "got labor religion" and courted the craft unions.[46] As Kaiser, even before the outbreak of war, was willing to pay any rate necessary to secure the best shipbuilding labor, the other Pacific Coast yards were forced to meet his price for skilled mechanics. This helped establish the government's wage-stabilization program on the West Coast, which was intended to prevent labor strife during the emergency. Eventually, journeymen carpenters and other skilled mechanics were paid $1.12 per hour.[47]

On the Pacific Coast, moreover, the AFL unions dominated and had closed-shop agreements in the yards, effectively shutting out the CIO, much to the chagrin of its leaders. This situation lasted until 1943, when the CIO unsuccessfully challenged the closed shop at the Kaiser yards in the courts.

The most overtly powerful labor figure in the shipyards was Tom Ray, the flamboyant business agent of the boilermakers. The vast numbers and great wealth of his locals put him in a position to run the yards. His downfall came in 1943, when he diverted dues to pay for an extravagant "labor temple" and private club he had ordered to be built. The club, as well as the union, barred women and blacks from entrance even though they were required to pay dues. They protested. Eventually, the national union relieved Ray of his duties.

The carpenters had their own influential figure in the yards—predictably, Bert Sleeman. In his own quiet way, he had greater influence in labor-management relations at the yards than Ray. Since the Depression, he had been a confidant of Edgar Kaiser, who had originally been sent to manage personnel affairs in Portland for the Bonneville project. The two men's friendship continued through the war years, and, Tom Ray notwithstanding, Sleeman was said to have been the real author of Oregon Ship's labor policies.[48] As two survivors of the era put it, "Bert Sleeman organized the shipyards his way."[49]

In practice, this meant that craft jurisdiction was generally respected; in particular, that carpenters' work remained under the control of the carpenters' union. This was a distinct accomplishment, considering that at Oregon Ship, the famous and constant innovations in the manufacturing process persistently blurred job descriptions and jurisdictional lines for the thirteen unions of the Pacific Coast Metal Trades Council, which still represented the shipyard crafts.[50]

On the other hand, Sleeman could do little about two related developments that adversely affected the Portland carpenters' locals in the postwar era. Even before Roosevelt's declaration of war, the AFL craft unions had been willing to relax standards in the yards in order to admit thousands of unskilled new workers to their ranks. This would help combat the growing labor shortage caused by the manpower needs of both the armed forces and the war industries. Unskilled workers were thus allowed to perform tasks ordinarily undertaken by first-class mechanics, the only stipulations being that they join the union and be paid journeyman's wages.[51]

With the boom in shipbuilding, job security was not threatened, the journeymen were generally needed as foremen and supervisors, and new recruits brought more money to the union's coffers. And with the closed or union shop in effect in most yards throughout the country, the unions did not view the new workers as tools of management, intended to weaken them.[52] The Portland yards thus saw hundreds of unskilled workers enter crafts for which they were fundamentally unprepared.

The degradation of craft standards at the shipyards that resulted was paralleled by the situation in regular construction. The new workers recruited by Oregon Ship to staff the round-the-clock shifts at the three Portland-area yards created an acute local housing shortage. The Housing Authority of Portland, created in 1941 to deal with the problem, authorized the accelerated construction of low-cost housing at a site on the Columbia Slough in North Portland, across from Vancouver, Washington. The community, known as Vanport, became the second largest community in Oregon, with over forty thousand residents and ten thousand housing units.

Again, for the carpenters' union, the significance of Vanport's construction lay not in the jobs it provided the locals, but in its delayed effect on craft standards. The chronic labor shortage in Portland caused two of the biggest subcontractors, the Gartrell and Buckler companies, to deliver to the Portland District Council of Carpenters an ultimatum: journeymen carpenters would be employed at Vanport as foremen, for foremen's wages, but crews would be made up of new hires (mostly Dust Bowl emigrants), who, like the new carpenters at the shipyards, were not union members and had not served apprenticeships.[53] The union could initiate these men or not as it wished, but the contractors would build with this labor, whatever the decision.[54]

The general-construction locals, particularly No. 226 and No. 583, were dismayed by the prospect of additional newcomers who could not pass the journeyman test. With no alternative to a flood of nonunion labor at the site, however, they acquiesced, and arranged to take the new workers into the union on special permits. The result was that, while their ranks were swelled (before World War II, there were between twelve hundred and fifteen hundred union carpenters in Portland; during the war, No. 226

alone had more than three thousand members), the quality of workmanship among carpenters declined as inexperienced craftsmen became card-
carrying journeymen. In the immediate postwar era, the epithet "shipyard" or "Vanport" carpenter indicated an inept workman.[55]

Two groups of wartime laborers benefited little from the sudden
opening of doors to new members. Women were assigned many jobs in
the shipyards, most notably as welders, but none found her way into the
carpenters' union. This pattern was true of shipyards across the United
States. By the same token, few of the eleven thousand blacks who came to
Portland for wartime employment found their way into the union. Those
who did were initiated with little incidence of overt racism.[56]

The end of the war in 1945 brought to a close a period of marked
economic contrasts for Portland's carpenters. The hardships of the Depression were juxtaposed with the full employment of the war years; the
half-empty union halls of the early thirties with the full membership ros-
ters of the carpenters' locals in the first years of the forties; the wage and
hour cutting, scrip, and WPA pay of lean times versus the fat pay envelopes
of the wartime shipyards.

While the carpenters and their leaders realized that this cycle of ex-
tremes was over, nobody had a clear vision of the future. Planning for the
postwar period had begun as early as 1943. In his Labor Day message to the
Oregon State Federation of Labor that year, Nickerson wrote that labor
leaders were "eagerly engaging with employing interests in a post-war
planning program to alleviate, or prevent, large scale unemployment."[57]
(Nickerson was among those appointed by Governor Earl Snell to the
state's postwar planning board.) At the level of the locals, discussions were
held at meetings on such topics as the role of carpenters in "pre-fab" housing construction.[58] The carpenters' locals had made efforts to retain members in the armed forces by paying their dues until their return and to
recruit new members by waiving initiation fees to veterans who presented
their discharge papers.[59]

In 1945, the future looked bright, if indistinct. The construction industry in Portland was almost completely organized in heavy and light
commercial construction, as well as home building, not only unionized,
but free of any CIO taint. The task was to make the most of peace and
prosperity.

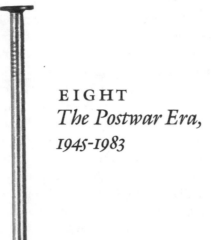

EIGHT
The Postwar Era,
1945-1983

THE POSTWAR ERA WAS ONE OF TRANS-
formation in every phase of the nation's life, especially in
economic and social affairs. Because in 1945 it was the
only major nation with its industrial plant left undamaged by the war, the
United States became the world's economic center. The subsequent expansion of the country's carrying capacity was a testament to that fact.
From 1932, when the gross national product was more than $58 billion, to
1960, when it was more than $503 billion, the economy grew nearly ten
times (at the war's conclusion, the GNP was more than $213.5 billion).[1] Still
better figures were to come, when in 1970 the GNP was recorded at over
$976 billion, and in 1978, in the midst of the "no-growth" epoch, at $2.633
trillion.[2]

Organized labor largely benefited from these developments. As the
work force grew in the postwar era, so, too, did unions. Union membership rose from 14.796 million in 1945 to 18.117 million in 1960 and 20.752

million in 1970.[3] In 1980, however, workers belonging to unions totaled 21.784 million, a figure representing a significant percentage decline because of the great growth of the total work force in the same period.[4]

The construction industry and its unions were especially favored by the expansion. The combination of the GI Bill, with its generous mortgage loan provisions, and the tremendous increase in the population in the twenty years after the war, created an unprecedented demand for housing that sustained contractors and workers alike for nearly thirty years. While the home-building boom eventually played out in the mid-seventies, general construction remained strong until the eighties, as federal, state, and local governments plunged into a huge program of upgrading, expansion, and replacement of the infrastructure of the United States. For example, the Highway Aid Act of 1956 funded construction of a network of about forty-one thousand miles of freeway, later extended by some fifteen hundred miles.[5]

After 1949, large cities as well as small towns became the beneficiaries or victims (depending on one's point of view) of massive destruction and construction of their cores. This was the result of the Housing Act, especially Title I of the law, which mandated federally subsidized slum clearance and public-housing construction. In addition, more dams, bridges, sewer lines, roads, mass-transit systems, schools, hospitals, and assorted public edifices were built with federal funds in the period from 1945 to 1983 than in the entire history of the republic.

In its initial stages, the postwar expansion was particularly helpful to West Coast unions. By 1960, unions on the Pacific Coast enjoyed greater-than-average membership; Washington was the most unionized state in the nation and Oregon was fifth.[6] Because the construction created boom jobs in wood-products manufacturing, and because the merger of the AFL and the CIO in 1955 helped stabilize the labor scene at the mills, the United Brotherhood of Carpenters was the largest union in Oregon. Indeed, the West Coast was the healthiest region within the brotherhood's orbit.[7]

In Portland, throughout the postwar period, the building trades, and in particular the carpenters, enjoyed relatively amicable and stable relations with employers. Among the reasons for this was that the area enjoyed an economic growth that fostered large and lucrative construction projects for most of the period until the late seventies. The wartime planning by the city's leaders for a transition to peacetime played a small role in this, but of greater importance was the city's attractiveness as a commercial and manufacturing venue. This was largely due to the relative cheapness of Portland's undeveloped industrial acreage and abundant power versus those of other West Coast cities.[8]

Portland, which with San Diego had sustained the greatest wartime expansion of all the Pacific Coast cities, experienced an enormous amount of industrial construction in the first two years after the war. A building for Willard Battery Company, two oil refineries, a fiberboard-products plant, a new facility for Quaker Oats, one for Pennsylvania Salt, and the expansion of the Oregon Portland Cement plant were indications of the health of the city's economy, as *Business Week* magazine pointed out.[9]

Certainly, these and other, lesser projects absorbed many of the former shipyard and Vanport carpenters who were affected by the all-but-total shutdown of the yards (following the pattern of World War I) at the conflict's end. Shipyard employment had plunged from a wartime high of 125,000 to approximately 3,000 in 1974.[10] Even though many former shipyard employees turned out, as previously noted, to be less than qualified, the flood tide of jobs kept most of those who remained in Portland on the union's rolls. This, in turn, contributed to the union's strength in the critical period of the late forties, when a shrinking membership might have put it in a defensive position. The union's hand was also strengthened by the house-building boom, which took hold in Portland as it did throughout the nation, persisting in its demands for manpower until the end of the sixties.

Succeeding years saw the carpenters' share in the general prosperity grow. Oregon received a significant portion of the federal largesse in the fifties and sixties. Federal highway monies funded 731 miles of separated roadways on three main routes in the state; four penetrating spurs and loops were also planned to serve Portland, Salem, and Eugene.[11] The first contracts of the estimated $650 million to be spent on the project were awarded in 1958.[12]

Bridges were integral to the highway system, and a parallel span to the Interstate Bridge over the Columbia between Vancouver and Portland was begun in 1956 and opened in 1960. Other bridge projects were the West Marquam Interchange, completed in 1966; the Fremont, opened in 1973; and the Glenn L. Jackson Bridge, which, like the Interstate, spanned the Columbia between Portland and Vancouver. It was finished in 1983. Monies for the interstate highway system were also dedicated for the improvement of such intra-urban spans as the Ross Island, Morrison, and Broadway bridges.

Although during the mid-seventies carpenters, in alliance with the Oregon AFL-CIO, the Associated General Contractors, and other interest groups, fought a hard but unsuccessful battle with Portland's then-mayor, Neil Goldschmidt, to build the Mt. Hood Freeway with federal funds appropriated for the purpose, the overall record in highway construction was highly beneficial to union members.[13] From the pilebucks of Local No. 2416 to the construction workers of No. 226 and No. 583, Portland's carpenters fanned out across the state on these projects for extended periods of time.

Similarly, the list of federally subsidized dam projects of the postwar years is a litany of good times for union carpenters. A series of River and Harbor acts passed by Congress beginning in 1945, as well as flood-control plans adopted by the Corps of Engineers, resulted in the construction of the McNary Dam, begun in 1947 and completed in 1955; The Dalles Dam, completed in 1959; and the John Day Dam, completed in 1968. This completed the damming of the Columbia along its Oregon shore.

Although made possible largely by the Flood Control Act of 1938, several projects on the Willamette and Santiam systems were not begun until after the war. They culminated in 1963, with the end of the Hills Creek Dam project on the middle fork of the Willamette.[14] Other dams in the series were Detroit and Big Cliff, its re-regulating dam on the North Santiam; and Lookout Point and its re-regulator, Dexter, on the middle fork of the Willamette. These were completed by 1960.[15]

In 1976, construction of the downtown Portland Transit Mall was begun with $16 million in funds provided by the U.S. Department of Transportation, the State of Oregon, and the City of Portland.[16] A light-rail line from Gresham to Portland was begun in 1982 with funds of $318 million from the same agencies.[17]

In the private sector, a number of large projects augmented the construction industry's postwar prosperity. Perhaps the centerpiece was the Lloyd Center project in northeast Portland, completed in 1960. At one time said to be the largest shopping mall in the world, it involved the construction of 1.3 million square feet of shopping space, a five-hundred-room hotel, and three office towers.[18]

Following a trend of suburbanization that became a major demographic feature of the era, major shopping complexes were begun in or near small cities and towns ringing Portland. These included Gateway and Eastport in east Multnomah County, completed in the early sixties; Washington Square near Tigard, completed in 1973; and the Clackamas Town Center, completed in 1981. The projects represented millions of dollars in wages for union carpenters.

Happily for contractors and carpenters alike, the retreat from the central city gave rise to yet another facet of the construction boom. Leading political, financial, and commercial figures in Portland sensed in the suburban flight a serious threat to the city's core. In the early fifties they therefore began a vigorous campaign for the area that required a mix of federal, state, local, and private funds. In the overall blueprint, the transit mall and the light-rail system figured prominently, but the main ingredients were an ambitious program of urban renewal centering around the Civic Auditorium at the downtown's south end. The project involved remodeling the auditorium as well as razing an entire neighborhood, and construction of a major hotel, five apartment towers, a small shopping mall, various office buildings, and a parking garage on the site.

Meanwhile, in Portland's downtown itself, the city's boosters were promoting Portland as a good site for regional or district headquarters. The subsequent explosion of office-tower construction in the sixties, seventies, and eighties produced such buildings as the First Interstate Bank Tower, opened in 1972; the U.S. Bank building of 1982; and the PacWest building, opened in 1984.

The municipal government of Portland also contributed to downtown construction, with the controversial Portland Building of 1982, an edifice of enduring architectural interest; and the Multnomah County Justice Center, which was opened in 1983.

This sustained activity in large-scale construction recalls the wartime setting of heavy production schedules requiring explicit and implicit cooperation between contractors and labor. Both had to be mindful of their mutual dependence in the face of a potentially long period of high profits and wages that could only be diminished by labor-management hostility.[19] After the war, too, both sides could draw on the exemplary tradition of cooperation established in the forties. So the imperative of maintaining the boom may have produced on both sides a willingness to nurture relative accord.[20]

Yet the tradition of amicability between carpenters and their employers was a recent and brief one. Moreover, neither side could confidently predict the future of the industry, for, despite all the construction, the national, regional, and local economies sent negative signals from time to time, as during the six postwar recessions. Either side might at any time see an advantage in breaking the accord. Other things must, therefore, have played a role in sustaining good relations.

One of these was the tradition of business unionism that prevailed among the locals of the Portland District Council of Carpenters after World War II. The general-construction locals, No. 226 and No. 583 in particular, continued to exert a heavy influence in the council's affairs, thanks to their large contributions to its annual budget and the fact that they were represented in its leadership by a series of able and articulate men. These included Sleeman (until his death in 1966), the elder statesman of the Building Trades Council; Swan Nelson, George Hahn, Clell Harris, Ed Weber, and Gerald Larsen. They and others, such as Roy Coles of the Pile Drivers, who served as executive secretary of the Oregon State Council of Carpenters from 1969 to 1979, remained solidly in the tradition of trade unionism fostered by Samuel Gompers and the old AFL. They were conservative, independent, bound to the values and order of a skilled craft, sure of the dignity of labor, and therefore, like their nineteenth-century predecessors, secure in a view of themselves as the equals of their employers.[21] The result was that few feelings of inferiority or class animosity existed to widen the gulf between management and labor.

The long association of the carpenters in the Oregon Building Congress provided a basis for exchanging views on the common problems of the industry in the Portland area. The atmosphere of candor, camaraderie, and mutual respect at the group's regular luncheon meetings through the years certainly contributed to the lack of strife.[22] When, in the eighties, the fabric of good relations in the industry began to fray somewhat under the stress of a sluggish economy (suggesting, perhaps, the significance of prosperity to the recipe for successful labor relations), the congress's role became more apparent. The shared despair or hope expressed at many meetings illustrated a recognition of the common destiny of the organization's elements.[23]

Perhaps key to maintaining good relations was the use of association bargaining in Portland during the postwar era. In such instances, a multiemployer bargaining group (the Associated General Contractors) and the five unions of the so-called raising trades (carpenters, laborers, teamsters, structural iron workers, and operating engineers) negotiate a master agreement that establishes basic employment standards. Although a form of association bargaining occurred in Portland as early as the turn of the century, the practice, as implemented in the Portland construction industry after 1945, originated in southern California in 1941.[24]

In a number of ways, association bargaining has served the peculiar interests of both sides, but in so doing, it has succeeded in reducing tensions, disputes, and misunderstandings that could lead to strikes. The floor under labor costs provided by the agreement, for example, has aided both labor and management by providing for craftsmen a reasonable minimum wage and, for contractors, the certainty that a competitor would not gain an advantage by undercutting labor standards. The concept has also helped individual employers by offering strength in numbers. The same is true for the building trades, which have undoubtedly gained more from contractors by collective action than they could by bargaining unilaterally. While there is no absolute test of this premise, a cursory examination of the wage scale of carpenters in the postwar years supports the assertion. Journeyman wages in construction in 1945 were $1.37 an hour. In 1983, at the union's centennial, they were at $16.19 per hour, a raw increase of 1,777 percent; the total package of compensation grew to include contributions by employers to medical, dental, pension, vacation, and various other funds.[25]

Association bargaining has also tended to diminish two of the more common problems of collective bargaining. One is the presence of extremists in either camp. The necessity of presenting a united front forces internal negotiations on each side before collective bargaining. This tends to produce a more moderate consensus on methods and goals in both camps, leading to smoother, less rancorous negotiations and earlier resolution than would be possible using the employer-by-employer method.[26]

The other problem that association bargaining ameliorates is that of interunion rivalries, which can lead to jurisdictional disputes and, consequently, work stoppages. By entering into a contract that systematically and comprehensively lays out comparative wage scales, craft jurisdiction, working conditions, and other variables of labor relations (such as relevant legislation, apprenticeship regulations, and movement of labor from one area to another), the building trades and their employers know in advance the role of each union at the construction site. This alone has been the basis of better relations among unions and between unions and contractors.[27]

It would be misleading to suggest that the postwar era could be characterized solely by the cooperative efforts of the various elements of the Portland area's construction industry. On the contrary, the years since 1945 have seen a fair measure of labor-management strife. Strikes occurred in home building in 1955 and in general construction in 1958. The pile drivers went on strike briefly in 1968. With some isolated actions among the mill locals, there were also various clashes between the union and management that nearly resulted in strikes.

The eighties, however, saw perhaps the most significant work stoppages. The deep distress of the Northwest economy during the first three years of the decade caused strained relations in all three segments of construction, shipbuilding, and wood-products milling. These strains symbolized critical problems throughout the trade that eclipsed the strikes or job actions themselves.

The strike in general construction was, in fact, informational picketing against the R.A. Hatch Company, a nonunion road builder. It began in the spring of 1983 and resulted in violence and bitterness. Hatch was the

lowest bidder by $2 billion against seven other companies on a segment of
the Banfield Freeway light-rail project.[28] The action was initiated by Local
No. 701 of the Operating Engineers, and the carpenters quickly joined.[29]
Although the recession had abated nationally, it was still severely affecting
Oregon, and hundreds of union construction workers had been without
jobs for a year or longer. Letting a contract (actually, one of a number that
had recently been won by Hatch) to such a company seemed unfair. Moreover, Hatch was accused of evading the Davis-Bacon Act by not paying
workers the prevailing local wage for various craft specialties. Hatch's
tactic, said union spokesmen, was to list workers for payroll purposes as
laborers at one pay rate when, in reality, they were actually doing other
kinds of work that by law required higher wages.[30]

The larger concern in the picketing, apart from the affront to the
carpenters and the other building trades, was that Hatch's success suggested a path other contractors might take in order to remain competitive in
the weak economy. Recent evidence had begun to show that such a pattern had already commenced. Nationally, the Associated General Contractors had initiated a campaign of antiunion militance.[31] A number of firms
with contracts in more than one state were operating in the so-called "dou-
ble-breasted" fashion—signing union contracts where necessary, using
the open shop where possible.[32] In Oregon, sixty-six contractors re-
nounced the master agreement in 1983. These included such major firms as
Donald M. Drake, Reimers and Jolivette, and H.A. Anderson.[33] The picketing of Hatch was thus a sign that, for the first time since the war, the
Building Trades were apprehensive about their position in the construction industry.[34]

The near-depression of 1980-82 also caused such severe dislocations in
the Northwest wood-products industry that, when renegotiations of the
Millworkers' contract came up in 1983, the eight largest West Coast mil-
lowners (bargaining as an association) felt justified not in attempting to
hold down wage increases, but in demanding "give-backs" of their workers. Wishing their employees to share in the effort to compete with southern u.s. and Canadian products, they advanced a contract that would cut
starting pay and either reduce paid holidays or trim fringe benefits.[35]

The unions—the Lumber Production and Industrial Workers of the

Carpenters Union and the International Woodworkers of America—agreed that workers should help the mills survive, but did not wish to forfeit the hard-won gains of the seventies. They called the issue of southern competition a "Trojan horse."[36] After a three-month strike, however, a settlement characterized by a one-year wage freeze followed by modest pay increases was negotiated with seven of the owners.

Only Louisiana-Pacific remained unsigned. The company refused the three-year pact, holding out for a one-year contract, an 8-10 percent cut in starting pay, and company-administered health benefits.[37] Using five hundred strikebreakers, Louisiana-Pacific operated eighteen plants at approximately 85 percent capacity. It closed its two least efficient plants.

Similarly, the strike in Portland's shipyards in the summer of 1983 was a sign of the weakness of the ship-repair industry and consequently of labor's bargaining position. Again, employers essentially demanded that the unions retreat from the gains made in the years after World War II. They offered a three-year wage freeze and an end to cost-of-living increases and health benefits, arguing that "cost containment," as they called it, was necessary if they were to compete with East Coast, Gulf Coast, and overseas shipyards.[38] The marine carpenters and the other crafts of the West Coast Metal Trades Council eventually walked out.

Although at the time of the strike the Port of Portland enjoyed a ship-repair business amounting to $140 million per year, private repair yards were in some difficulties. Unarguably, the domestic shipbuilding and repair business had suffered throughout the years since the war's end for many reasons, including the large inventory of floating stock in the form of Liberty and Victory ships available at bargain prices after the conflict and the rise of Japan and South Korea as shipbuilding centers. Indeed, in 1956, the last two vessels wholly constructed in Portland slipped down the ways. These were two Matson Line cruise ships, the *Mariposa* and the *Monterey*.[39] In later years, competition from Gulf Coast yards operating under the open shop played a role in the dearth of business, as did the allocation of Navy contracts to those yards, often obtained by states whose congressmen had influence in the Pentagon.

The general weakness of the industry on the West Coast, exacerbated once again by the recession, forced the confrontation as management grasped at straws to deal with its problems. However, the attempt to force concessions on workers proved impractical, as the strike diverted ships in need of repair to yards in the Far East and elsewhere. On 27 September 1983, therefore, both sides signed a compromise agreement ending the strike.[40] The three-year duration of the contract promised to be only a stopgap for an industry with structural ills.

The generally positive postwar balance in Portland's construction industry, between good labor-management relations on the one hand and significant employer-union strife on the other, does not adequately portray the carpenters' situation during the period, particularly in the two decades before their centennial in 1983. At least two chronic and complex difficulties beset the union in these years. Nor were these minor irritations. Instead, they represented real threats to the future strength and vigor of the construction locals. As the union's hundredth anniversary approached, these difficulties remained largely unresolved.

One of the problems was that of manpower replacement or, more specifically, apprenticeship and training. As Portland's carpenters had always realized, organizing and maintaining craftsmen with the greatest skill was the best defense against the erosion of their bargaining position and the triumph of the open shop. Consequently, an active, vigorous, and productive apprenticeship program was seen as essential to the health of the union. In the years after World War II, this need was heightened by the persistence of the "shipyard" carpenters, who continued to ply the trade despite inferior skills, both in and out of the union, providing manpower for nonunion contractors or sullying the locals' reputation for craftsmanship in the union shops. Yet, despite an awareness of the importance of apprenticeship—locals No. 226 and No. 583 had always been the strongest supporters of the concept, as we have seen—the carpenters showed a disturbing inability to attract adequate numbers of new workers to their ranks in the years after 1945.

This dilemma was not confined to Portland. A dearth of apprentices beset nearly all skilled crafts across the United States at the time. In 1949, the Department of Labor estimated that replacements needed to maintain the pool of skilled labor at a constant level were between 3 and 5 percent of the work force.[41] In the building trades, however, only one-fourth of the individuals represented by those percentages registered in apprenticeship programs.[42] This situation was further aggravated by the fact that apprenticeship programs could turn out only about one-fourth of their enrollees each year.[43] Moreover, the requirements of the national emergency had curtailed or postponed serious training programs, so that such programs accounted for only about 9 percent of the increase in skilled labor from 1940 to 1948.[44] Clearly, the entire nation began the reconversion from war to peace with a definite shortage of skilled manpower.

Thus, in Portland as elsewhere, the carpenters' apprenticeship policies took on a special significance. From the beginning of the postwar era, the carpenters, with the building trades as a whole, emphasized their active concern and support for apprenticeship as one of their most important responsibilities.[45] In the early 1950s, Lloyd Goodwin, the carpenters' apprenticeship coordinator, worked indefatigably to maintain and publicize the apprenticeship program, as well as refresher courses on such subjects as blueprint reading and the use of the steel square for journeymen.[46] However, there was a charge for the classes (thirty cents an hour in 1950), and enrollment ran consistently low; Goodwin lobbied for free classes. On 1 May 1965, his goal was achieved when the union and management established an apprenticeship training trust. Contributions from the carpenters beginning at two cents per compensable hour per member increased to twelve cents in 1989 to cover apprentices' training costs.[47]

In 1950, with concern over the state of training running high, the carpenters were active in bringing together employers, labor representatives, and elected officials from the eleven western states for a conference on apprenticeship. Oregon's governor, Douglas McKay, speaking before an audience that included some of his fellow state executives, noted that Oregon had "one of the best apprenticeship programs in the nation, especially in the building trades unions."[48] One exhibit at the conference was a letter from employers to Bert Sleeman written in 1920, thanking the carpenters for their active and sustained participation in apprenticeship programming.

The praise, although welcome, did little to solve the chronic problem with which apprenticeship training was intended to deal. The carpenters and the Building Trades Council therefore continued to fine-tune the program in all its aspects. For example, in 1951, the statewide Building Trades Convention passed a resolution that all employer members of the State Apprenticeship Council must have at least one year's experience in hiring apprentice labor and that labor members must have worked in the trade they represented or in a relevant apprentice program.[49] The purpose of this was to eliminate representation on the council by trade association executives with no intimate knowledge of the problems involved.[50]

Later in the year, Goodwin, in cooperation with the State Trades Council, worked to standardize training procedures. As a result, a booklet delineating the United Brotherhood of Carpenters' training program was adopted as the standard training manual in the craft for the State of Oregon.[51] The extent of concern for the state of carpentry was indicated by a companion proposal for an extensive program for journeymen.[52]

Again in 1951, apprenticeship training was important enough to warrant three locations at which to attend class in the Portland metropolitan area: at 220 Northeast Beech Street in Portland and in Hillsboro and Oregon City. "Attending school regularly is a MUST for apprentices if you want to work on the job," read one notice in the *Labor Press*.[53] At the close of a year, forty-five carpenter apprentices graduated from the school, having taken four years of classes totaling one hundred and forty-four hours of instruction.

The carpenters tried to stimulate enrollment in the program in many different ways; these included various apprentice contests, replete with attractive prizes, for the greatest displays of craftsmanship. Nevertheless, by the end of the decade, there was every indication that the shortage of skilled workers was becoming critical. In 1959 Andrew Sears of Local No. 226, representative to the State Apprenticeship Council, observed that, in the entire state, there were only 163 carpenter apprentices.[54] He estimated that the number should be ten times greater. "It's getting hard these days," he said, "to find a good all-around carpenter who can do all the things a carpenter is supposed to do."[55]

The shortage was even more acute in the next decade. This was because there were more older journeymen than there had ever been (the average age of Oregon's twelve thousand journeymen in 1962 was fifty-two), while in that same year, only eighteen apprentices completed training.[56] Assuming a normal rate of attrition, fourteen hundred apprentices were required, with three hundred graduating each year.[57] A carpenter familiar with the state of affairs claimed that the training program was inadequate, that the graduates were not even fully qualified, and that twice as many apprentices left the program of their own accord or were dropped before completing training as the number who actually finished the program. While some of them lacked an aptitude for carpentry and went on to other careers, many returned to the trade as nonunion journeymen.[58]

As always, many solutions were proposed. The State Council of Carpenters Apprenticeship Committee requested that a fund be instituted for a program to coordinate training facilities and to publicize the need for training of more apprentices.[59] One proposal conceded defeat on the issue of numbers, while confronting the quality of trainees directly. The idea was to establish a preapprenticeship program in high school and at jobsites that would select only those with real potential who were likely to complete the full course.[60]

These initiatives never reached fruition largely because of a shortage of funds, but on a more modest scale, No. 226 began its own experiment to encourage young people to enter the trade. In order to foster pride of craftsmanship among members' sons, in 1965 the local began a competition in industrial arts and crafts. Contestants entered a variety of school shop projects in wood, copper, and ceramics. The winners were honored at a meeting of the union and given savings bonds and cash as prizes.[61] The *Labor Press* praised the effort as vital to the health of the crafts.[62]

In the mid-1960s the whole question took on greater significance when, in the wake of social and political developments that included the civil-rights and anti-Vietnam war movements, there began an intensive examination of economic opportunity in the United States. Many critics concluded that ethnic minorities and women had been barred systematically from economic advancement.[63] Because they were usually ineligible, for various reasons, to obtain assistance from large financial institutions to start businesses of their own or to join a union controlling jobs in highly skilled crafts, the disadvantaged would always remain so, unless aggressive action were taken to ensure their participation in the economy.

The building trades were a particular target of activists in this regard.

Some of the crafts had behaved as if they were the exclusive preserves of white males. The boilermakers of the Portland shipyards during World War II were a case in point. But on 21 June 1963, eighteen building trades unions agreed with the government to end discrimination in employment.[64] Although it had a generally good record in civil rights, the United Brotherhood of Carpenters signed the agreement and moved quickly to implement the policy. The union's General Executive Board issued a statement that acknowledged racial segregation in some locals and promised to eradicate it.[65] William Hutcheson told the secretary of labor, "We are interested in wiping out all discrimination based on race, creed, or color in job opportunities and you may rest assured we will continue our efforts to achieve this goal."[66]

The key to greater participation by members of minority groups lay in proper preparation through apprenticeship. A drive to recruit trainees, and to educate employers (who, as Hutcheson pointed out, bore a measure of responsibility for the problem in their own hiring practices), was therefore undertaken. The most important steps in recruiting minorities into the skilled crafts, however, were taken by the Johnson administration in its war on poverty. Through the Comprehensive Education and Training Act of 1967, the Job Corps, and various other programs that came under the general heading of the Economic Opportunity Act of 1964, thousands of disadvantaged youths were given access to the skilled crafts throughout the next decade.

In Portland, there was no resistance from the carpenters' locals to comply with the letter and spirit of the agreement. This was in part because there were at least a few black union members after World War II and, more significantly, because they represented only some 4.5 percent of the city's work force by 1975.[67] There were never significant numbers of them to be assimilated into the union. In 1976, thirteen years after the inception of the major antipoverty programs, only slightly more than 1 percent of the metropolitan area's total employed black workforce was listed as "construction craftsmen."[68] This figure represented 129 persons spread among the five major crafts of the building trades and thirteen subcrafts.

Portland's carpenters became active in bringing young people who were members of minority groups or who were otherwise disadvantaged into the trade. In 1968 the United Brotherhood of Carpenters chose Oregon as the site of a program contracted with the federal government to train such young people. At Timber Lake near Estacada, the Forest Service ran a Job Corps camp where apprenticeship training was available. Students earned the equivalent of a high-school diploma and the chance to learn the craft under Chuck Miller, president of No. 226, and carpenters from the Portland locals.[69] The first class graduated in September 1968. The students returned to the civilian world as trained apprentices, ready to assume jobs leading to journeyman status.

Unfortunately, the Timber Lake program had no direct impact on Portland's shortage of skilled craftsmen. Almost all the students were from elsewhere in the United States—the majority from California and the deep South—and returned to their homes to seek work when their training was over. A program designed to reach Portland's black population produced one black apprentice in three months of recruitment.[70] Only fifteen people had expressed any interest in the program. Timber Lake, meanwhile, continues to operate as a preapprenticeship training center where "hard-core" unemployed young people are given a chance to learn work skills, taught by union carpenters.

Even as the carpenters and other building trades attempted to improve affirmative action in the construction industry for blacks and members of other minority groups, women began to move into the work force in greater numbers than ever before and to break down most of the stereotypes about their occupational capabilities. Some gravitated to carpentry. In Portland, despite the example of women in the shipyards during World War II, they were not readily accepted by the locals, and at least one female journeyman, Kate Barrett of No. 247, describes her attempts to enter the union in 1971 as a long, frustrating series of visits to various locals where her efforts were thwarted by indifferent or hostile men.[71] Finally, in 1975, after several years of working at carpentry in nonunion shops, she thought it imperative that she join an apprenticeship program to improve her skills. She therefore made another effort to join the union and was accepted without hesitation. Eventually, she became the first woman in the state to qualify through the apprenticeship program as a journeyman carpenter.[72]

In 1982, she became a trustee of Local No. 226. In 1983, she was one of perhaps twenty-five women in the various locals throughout Portland.[73]

Clearly, including members of minority groups and women has not solved the apprenticeship crisis. There are too few of either to make a real difference. The crisis of numbers thus lingered into the decade of the eighties.

Another difficulty faced by Portland's union carpenters in the years since the end of World War II has been the impact of technological change: in construction techniques, as in the greater use of tilt-up walls; in architectural practices and standards, as in the increased reliance on exposed beams in houses and red iron in commercial structures; in materials, as in the substitution of metal studs and joists for wooden ones; in tools, as in the replacement of the hammer by the nail gun. Many more such changes could be documented, but the point is that all the recent changes have had an effect on the carpenter's task at the construction site, whether to shorten the length of time required to complete it, or perhaps even to eliminate the task.

Nowhere is the impact of technological change on union carpentry in the postwar era more apparent than in the field of home building. In this segment of the construction industry, the once-dominant union lost its grip, due in large measure because of its inability to deal with the consequences of technological change. While the union has relinquished its capacity to organize home building in much of the rest of the country for similar reasons, the fact is more significant in Portland because other construction has remained so highly organized in the city. Walter Galenson, historian of the United Brotherhood of Carpenters, has written that of the cities best organized in industrial and commercial construction, but unorganized in home building, Denver, Kansas City, and Portland provide the most vivid examples.[74]

Why did this occur? Social and economic transformations played a large role in the loss of home building, but only insofar as they were inextricably linked to technological change. In the years immediately after the war, the steady expansion of the home-building industry attracted established prewar union contractors who stayed competitive through volume sales, reasonably stable costs, skilled and productive crews, and consequently manageable per-unit and per-square-foot costs.[75] They formed a basis for a unionized environment in the industry.

In the late sixties and seventies, however, the slackening of demand for housing in Oregon—occasioned by a diminishing birthrate and lower immigration, rising interest rates, and chronic inflation from 1966 to 1982 —changed Portland's home-building industry dramatically. Contract negotiations between the building trades and the Homebuilders' Association in 1969 were perhaps the last meaningful ones held in the city. After this, union contractors dwindled to a handful.[76]

The industry's transformation may appear to be attributable to the changes in social and economic circumstances. Inevitably, these changes led to an intensification of competition because of the shrinking market and lower profit margins resulting from higher per-square-foot costs.[77] Still, the years 1972 and 1978 were the two best for the postwar home-building industry in Portland. In 1972 in the metropolitan area, 20,500 housing units were constructed; in 1978, just under 20,000.[78] By 1982, in the depths of the recession, the statistic was 6,700 units, the worst postwar performance.[79] The carpenters' union figured little in any of these.

Neither economics nor social patterns can entirely account for this. Instead, two developments related to each other and to technological change pushed the union out of the industry. The first of these was the fragmentation of the home-building crafts, stemming from the rise of new materials and techniques designed to cut costs and increase productivity in the industry. These included the use of sheetrock in place of lath and plaster, metal window and door frames instead of wood, "stand-up" framing construction, metal siding, prefabricated roof systems, and the increased use of carpeting and other synthetic flooring materials in place of hardwood. These materials and techniques required merely a limited understanding of a particular phase of the construction process and an ability to work with a material usually more forgiving of imprecision than wood.[80] They did not require the sophisticated training procedures of apprenticeship, but merely an introduction to the apprentice's duties and tools. This new breed of workers, whose existence was predicated almost wholly on technological advancement, proved to be cost-efficient and productive. Ironically, the workers' new techniques and materials and the innovative system of production in which they labored took them back to the nineteenth century in their relationship to their jobs and their employers. They had become the new pieceworkers.

The second development was the rise of "checkbook contractors."[81] Recognizing the nature of the transformation of the home-building industry, they were not primarily builders with their own permanent crew of workers, interested as much in the processes of construction as in the marketing of the final product, but coordinators of various subcontractors who wished to bring a competitively priced house to market as speedily and cheaply as possible. They had no payrolls of their own to maintain and no responsibilities to traditional standards of construction, aside from those imposed by local building codes. In short, they orchestrated and reinforced the fragmentation of the craft of home building.

The industry, both nationally and locally, had traditionally been diverse and cyclical. Despite the prolonged postwar stability and the presence in the market of large traditional contractors during the first two decades after the war, there had always been a high proportion of small builders who moved in or out of the market depending on conditions. No local figures are available, but at the national level as early as 1949, 80 percent of all building firms started fewer than five houses, and about 50 percent started one house each.[82] Most of these firms were active for only part of the year or did residential building only as a sideline.[83]

In the diminished circumstances of home building in Portland through most of the seventies and early eighties, nearly all the traditional builders abandoned the market to the new breed of contractors, who thus constituted almost all the home builders in the Portland area. Because they were not employers in the true sense of the word, it was hard for business agents to deal with them.[84] They were also in and out of the industry, so they were sometimes even hard to find.

By the same token, their subcontractors were frequently self-employed, independent workers who saw themselves as their own bosses, rather than as employees needing the protection of a union.[85] They, too, proved hard for business agents to deal with.

For the union's part, it became increasingly difficult to define all the tasks in the new home building that constituted part of the craft of carpentry.[86] Despite the dictum of Peter McGuire, laid down almost at the birth of the United Brotherhood of Carpenters, that "Once wood, it is always the right of the carpenter to install it, no matter what the material now used may happen to be," the occasions for jurisdictional disputes with other trades proliferated and further complicated the task of policing the industry.[87]

Rank-and-file carpenters themselves lost enthusiasm for jobs in home building when postwar trends in wage negotiations began to produce unfavorable differentials between pay in the field as against commercial construction.[88] Gradually, the union's will to keep the industry organized eroded. As one construction industry analyst interpreted the event, the union had simply decided to "write off" home building rather than attempt to remain competitive through wage concessions.[89]

Finally, the market itself spoke on the subject of unionization. Its vote was unfavorable. In the East and Midwest throughout the postwar era, tract houses—small (typically one thousand square feet), largely identical, mass-produced units, with many of their components produced off-site— were highly saleable. The example of Levittown in Pennsylvania, with its acres of sprawling sameness, comes to mind. Portlanders, however, have traditionally preferred larger, more distinctive dwellings, making each house something of a personal statement.[90] In the seventies, new Portland homes averaged twelve hundred square feet; by the eighties, fifteen hundred.[91] These essentially "custom-built" homes have raised the total cost of individual houses. Contractors, trying to keep such houses at competitive prices, therefore resisted the union on the assumption that lower, nonunion wages would keep their prices down.[92]

Here again, technological change played a role in the carpenters' affairs. The ability to mass-produce homes, the product of technological advances, could have saved the industry or the union. Indeed, in the mid-sixties two companies, u.s. Homes and Centex, tried to market factory housing in Portland. They were met with resounding indifference.[93] With their exodus from the city went the only hope for a substantial union foothold in Portland home building as the centennial of the union approached.

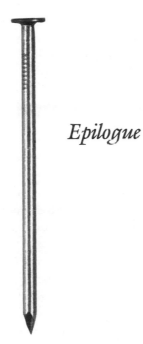

Epilogue

ON THE EVENING OF 22 SEPTEMBER 1983, at the old Local No. 583 hall in North Portland, a gathering was held to commemorate one hundred years of union carpentry in the City of Portland. The hall smelled of freshly applied paint that lightened the large meeting room where more than two hundred carpenters, their families, and various guests and dignitaries had congregated. Otherwise, the surroundings were spartan in appearance, and the gaiety was subdued.

A play, *Builders of the Nation*, originally produced for the United Brotherhood of Carpenters' centennial in 1981, was performed. The story it told of the union over the century of its existence was a moving tableau of the brotherhood's struggles. Later, experts on labor history, economics, and carpenters' union affairs presented their views of the union's future. It was, in the aggregate, a portrait forecasting more problems for the Portland locals and their members. The historian David Johnson put the carpenters' history into the context of the long saga of labor in the United States and pointed out the signs of a "continuing secular decline in both numbers and organized power of labor," as well as the necessity of adjustment by labor unions to the "'new,' increasingly technologically based, service oriented economy."[1] The economist Ray Broughton spoke of an arduous transition from high interest rates and inflated currency to a more friendly banking atmosphere for investors and sounder money for consumers that would catalyze a return to prosperity.[2] He thought this would bring hardship to many union members for some time. Mark Furman, a regional official of the United Brotherhood of Carpenters, diagnosed the loss of jobs in the building trades as a function of the continuing movement of American manufacturers to offshore sites. He called the export of American jobs a problem that would not soon abate.[3]

If the occasion seemed somewhat austere, there was good reason for it. In the previous year, locals No. 226, No. 583, and No. 1020 had merged to form No. 247, largely because of dwindling membership in all three.[4] At the height of the postwar prosperity, No. 226 alone had reached a high of approximately twenty-five hundred members. In 1983, in the depths of recession, the new, combined local's membership was about twenty-one hundred. Among active members, the average total annual working hours was 785. In good years, the average would have been twice that figure. Many of those out of work had been jobless for a protracted period. Some had run out of unemployment benefits and were forced to live on welfare.

There were other bad signs. A study released in July 1982 by the Oregon Chapter of the Associated General Contractors showed that union contractors were finding it more and more difficult to compete against nonunion firms. The study's editor flatly told the *Oregonian* that, as contractors moved in growing numbers to the open shop in order to survive, unions would become a thing of the past.[5] He cited as evidence of this trend the fact that in 1978, unions controlled 79 percent of all construction contracts in Oregon and southwest Washington, with 21 percent in the hands of open-shop contractors.[6] At the close of 1981, however, the union share was down to 54 percent.[7] Furthermore, said the study, the building trades were ensuring their demise by refusing to negotiate lower wages and eliminating restrictive conditions where circumstances demanded such concessions in order to remain competitive.

Nevertheless, there was much about which the audience could be positive on the carpenters' hundredth anniversary. The speakers' realism was tempered by genuine optimism. Johnson spoke of the sustaining power of the labor movement's time-tested ideals in its quest for social and economic justice. Broughton sketched a strong future role for the union, founded on the enduring principles of trade unionism. He predicted that, with the return of a strong dollar, a new emphasis on the necessity of craftsmanship and honest effort would reanimate the crafts and cause employers and workers alike to seek out the carpenters' union as the great breeding ground and medium of those principles. The high productivity rates of union workers, he said, gave strong evidence of the significance of organized labor to the nation's economic future.[8]

Furman predicted that the building trades would be capable of executing necessary adjustments in makeup and jurisdiction in the face of the radical changes in technology. New jobs in the building trades would be found not at construction sites, but in factories, where prefabricated structures would be manufactured. Moreover, he remained sanguine about the value of labor organizations and collective bargaining. There would always be a particular place for unions as long as management continued to "squeeze everything for the stockholders."[9] "Management," he observed, "creates the need for a union. We'll be there when the time comes."[10]

The Portland locals had already begun the process of adjusting to the future. The carpenters, with other building trades unions, were charter members of the Pacific Northwest Finance Forum, an organization designed to combat the construction slump by using the locals' pension trusts to generate new construction projects. By lending their combined funds to finance mortgages on important new projects, the unions hoped to put many of their members back to work. Naturally, union contractors and union labor would be stipulated on any loan agreement. The forum hoped to be able to tap as much as $400 million of pension monies for use as loan funds.[11]

At the same time, steps were being taken to rethink and reforge the relationship between the carpenters and their employers. In August 1983, the State District Council of Carpenters, successor to the Portland District Council, received a grant of $64,627 from the Federal Mediation and Conciliation Service, to fund an eighteen-month project that would "promote cooperation between union contractors and workers with the goal of providing the best quality work for consumers."[12] Specifically, the grant called for a committee made up of five representatives of the carpenters' locals and five representatives of management to develop workshops, seminars, and one demonstration construction project. On the project, the committee planned to introduce "quality circles" at the construction site, in an effort to create opportunities for labor and management to improve communications and cooperation on the job.[13]

The theme that emerged from the centennial evening's events seemed to be one of struggle: the struggle of the pioneers of union carpentry to overcome inequities in the workplace; the struggle of the Portland locals in the eighties to maintain the hard-won achievements of a hundred years; the struggle promised in the next hundred to extend the gains of the past, to adapt to technological change, to continue to strengthen the social and economic fabric of the city. It was a reminder that the labor movement was born of struggle, that the great goals of labor—the eight-hour day, the living wage, the universal recognition of the dignity of work—had been achieved only through struggle, that it was the task of the union carpenters of Portland to continue to strive in their own behalf. It was a reminder that they had been an integral part of the struggle to build the Portland of the past and that they would once again be required to struggle if they were to be builders of its future.

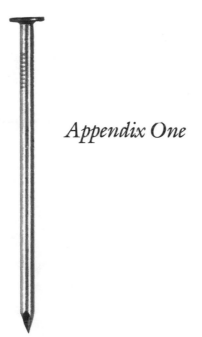

Appendix One

UNION CARPENTERS' WAGES AND BENEFITS
IN PORTLAND, OREGON, 1883-1984
(Entire Wage Package Not Shown)

1883—1955

YEAR	WAGES Per Day	Per Hour	Foreman's Differential
1883	$3.00 (9-10 hours)		
1890	3.50 (8 hours)		
1915	4.00		
1916	4.00		
1917	5.60		
1918	5.60		

YEAR	WAGES Per Day	Per Hour	Foreman's Differential
1919	8.00		
1920	8.00		
1921	7.20		
1922	8.00		
1923	8.00		
1924	8.00		
1925	8.00		
1926	9.00		
1927	9.00		
1928	9.00		
1929	9.00		
1930	9.00		
1931	9.00		
1932	7.20		
1933	5.40		
1934	7.20		
1935	7.20		
1936	8.00		
1937	9.00		
1938	9.00		
1939	9.00		
1940	9.00		
1941		$1.20	
1942		1.35	$1.00 more/day
1943		1.35	1.00 more/day
1944		1.375	
1945		1.375	
1946		1.55	
1947		1.75	
1948		1.925	2.00 more/day
1949		2.10	2.00 more/day
1950		2.10	2.00 more/day

YEAR	WAGES Per Day	Per Hour	Foreman's Differential
1951		2.25	2.00 more/day
1952		2.45	.125 more/hour
1953		2.55	2.00 more/day
1954		2.75	.25 more/hour
1955		2.75	.25 more/hour

1956-1984

DATE	WAGES Per Hour	Foreman's Differential	BENEFITS (per hour) H&W	Dental	Pension
Jan. 1956	$2.80	$.25	$.10		
Jan. 1957	2.90	.25	.10		
Jan. 1958	3.10	.25	.10		
Apr. 1959	3.28	.25	.10		
Apr. 1960	3.46	.25	.10		
Apr. 1961	3.63	.25	.10		
Apr. 1962	3.83	.50	.10		
Jun. 1962	3.73	.50	.10		.10
Apr. 1963	3.83	.50	.15		.15
May 1965	4.33	.50	.15		.15
May 1966	4.68	.50	.15		.15
May 1967	5.03	.50	.15		.15
May 1968	5.10	.50	.25		.20
May 1969	5.58	.50	.25		.25
May 1970	6.03	.50	.25		.25
June 1971	6.28	.50	.30	.05	.30
Dec. 1971	6.38	.50	.35	.05	.35
June 1972	6.78	.50	.40	.15	.40
June 1973	7.29	.60	.40	.15	.40
June 1974	7.79	.60	.40	.15	.65
June 1975	8.79	.60	.40	.15	.65
Oct. 1975	9.29	.60	.40	.15	.65

DATE	WAGES Per Hour	Foreman's Differential	BENEFITS (per hour) H&W	Dental	Pension
June 1976	10.09	.60	.40	.15	.65
June 1977	10.65	.60	.40	.15	.85
June 1978	11.28	.60	.45	.15	.95
June 1979	12.12	.60	.65	.15	1.00
June 1980	13.80	.65	.85	.15	1.00
June 1981	15.12	.65	.85	.15	1.10
June 1982-84	16.19	.65	1.10	.15	1.10

1985-1988

DATE	WAGES Per hour	FRINGE BENEFITS
June 1985	16.31	4.02
June 1986	17.02	4.02
June 1987	17.02	3.67
June 1988	17.60	3.84

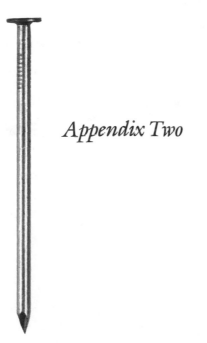

Appendix Two

PORTLAND LOCALS OF THE
UNITED BROTHERHOOD OF CARPENTERS,
1883-1983*

NOTE: Local 1266, a general-construction local, is not listed in United Brotherhood of Carpenters files; however, its existence in the second decade of the twentieth century is generally accepted. Local 1266 may have consolidated with 1106 at some point. Both served southeast Portland (Sellwood, East and West Moreland).

Locals that, for a variety of reasons, disband, are required to return the official charter and seal to the international. On a number of occasions in the history of Portland's United Brotherhood of Carpenters locals, this

*Data in tables are from files of General Office, UNITED BROTHERHOOD OF CARPENTERS, Washington, D.C.

procedure was not followed, usually as a result of neglect. Therefore, the list of defunct locals has a variety of notations reflecting the diligence of the officials in closing down the operations.

Suspension of a local results when a local fails to pay its per capita tax on the membership to the international.

Beneficial and semi-beneficial status refer to a distinction in retirement and death benefit structures between construction locals and lumber industry locals (Lumber Production Industrial Workers) and millmen locals. Construction locals enjoy full benefits administered by the international, while Lumber Production Industrial Workers and millmen do not receive death benefits through the United Brotherhood of Carpenters but through the regional bodies of their own.

LOCAL NUMBER	DATE CHARTERED	REMARKS
50	9/22/1883	See 226, 3/8/16
1450	2/21/1903	Charter returned 1/6/04
1673	4/28/04	Consolidated with 50 in 1905
1638	4/30/04	Consolidated with 1673 in 1905
808	6/1/08	See 226, 3/8/16
1120	2/23/12	Millmen; consolidated with 2009, 3/12/73
1937	3/24/13	Hardwood floor layers; consolidated with 226, 2/5/18
583	5/6/13	Consolidated with 247, 9/1/82
1106	5/20/13	Consolidated with 226, charter and seal returned, 9/12/33
1052	10/30/13	Caulkers; suspended 9/19/19; former members transferred to 2218, 3/6/20
872	12/15/13	Bridge dock and pier carpenters; disbanded in 1916
1020	12/15/13	Shipwrights and joiners; suspended by general president, 9/18/19
2543	1/8/14	Formed 2154 in 1923
226	3/8/16	50 and 808 consolidated to form 226
1540	2/2/18	Millwrights; consolidated with 1120, 4/19
2218	7/22/19	Consolidated with 1020, 4/27/71
1020	3/10/20	Shipwrights and joiners; reorganized and consolidated with 583 and 226, 9/1/82

LOCAL NUMBER	DATE CHARTERED	REMARKS
2416	3/17/20	Pile drivers, dock and wharf builders
2154	3/31/24	Lathers' local
1482	3/26/34	Changes to semibeneficial 3182 4/43; charter returned 9/16/41
3182	3/26/34	Consolidated with Millmen's Local 3067 of Albany, Oregon, no date.
2531	4/11/35	Started beneficial status 4/49; consolidated with 2281, 1/31/79
2532	4/12/35	Disbanded, 1940
2543	4/16/35	Disbanded, 1940
2553	4/22/35	Charter returned 9/28/37
2597	5/20/35	Consolidated with 2531, no date
2612	5/28/35	Consolidated with 2881, 9/58
1746	7/18/35	Millmen; formed from 1120 membership
2658	8/14/35	Disbanded, charter and seal returned, 11/29/37
2672	9/3/35	Consolidated with 2532, 1/37
2651	9/14/36	Disbanded, 1937
2882	2/8/37	Disbanded, 1/40
2883	2/8/37	Disbanded, 1/40
1537	3/8/37	Charter returned, 9/16/41
1777	4/12/37	Suspended, 1/49
2839	8/26/37	Disbanded, charter returned, 12/14/45
2877	2/2/38	Consolidated with 2881, 12/53
2878	2/3/38	Consolidated with 2881, 12/53
2879	2/3/38	Consolidated with 2281, 12/53
2880	2/3/38	Consolidated with 2881, 12/53
2881	2/8/38	Consolidated with 2531, 1/31/79
2884	2/8/38	Disbanded, 1/40
738	11/7/40	Consolidated with 3182, 5/17/34
2969	8/25/41	Formed with charter of disbanded 2543; consolidated with Kalama, Washington, Local 2755, no date.
2937	11/27/41	Disbanded, charter retired, 2/15/44
1857	6/23/47	Suspended, 1/49
247	6/30/82	Consolidated with 583, 1020, 9/1/82

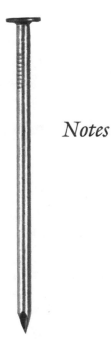

Notes

CHAPTER ONE   Beginnings

1. I have relied on Joseph Gaston, *Portland: Its History and Builders*, vol. 1 (Chicago: S.J. Clarke Publishing Company, 1911), 609, as the basis for this figure. Gaston cites 17,577 as Portland's population in 1880 and quotes 46,385 as the population for 1890. Commentary from this author and others suggest that the rapid growth during the decade occurred as a result of the arrival of the transcontinental line. I have therefore made an educated guess about the expansion of the city's population to that point by employing a calculation from the standard deviation. It should be pointed out that J.K. Gill's *Portland City Directory, 1882* (Portland: George Himes Press, 1882), 42, cites the city's population as 17,578 for that year, an increase of one over the federal census of 1880. Gill's 1883 edition cavalierly dropped the statistical section.

2. *See* John R. Commons et al., *History of Labor in the United States*, vol. 1 (New York: Macmillan Co., 1918), Matthew Josephson, *The Robber Barons* (New York: Harcourt Brace, 1934), Herbert Gutman, *Work, Culture and Society in Industrializing America* (New York: Alfred A. Knopf, 1976), and Samuel

Gompers, *Seventy Years of Life and Labor*, 2 vols. (New York: Dutton, 1957), for a general background of the American labor movement in the nineteenth century.

See Dorothy O. Johansen and Charles M. Gates, *Empire of the Columbia*, 2nd ed. (New York: Harper & Row, 1967), 348-50, 479-85; Gordon B. Dodds, *Oregon: A History* (New York: W.W. Norton, 1977), chs. 3-5; E. Kimbark MacColl, *The Shaping of a City, Business and Politics in Portland, Oregon, 1885-1915* (Portland: The Georgian Press, 1976), chs. 1-6, for an overview of Pacific Northwest, Oregon, and Portland economic development and labor organization to the end of the nineteenth century. Jack Triplett, "History of the Oregon Labor Movement Prior to the New Deal" (Master's thesis, University of California, Berkeley, 1961), focuses mostly on early Portland unions.

The early history of the carpenters' union, the United Brotherhood of Carpenters and Joiners of America, is covered in a scholarly way in Walter Galenson, *The United Brotherhood of Carpenters, The First Hundred Years* (Cambridge: Harvard University Press, 1983), and in an informal history by Thomas Brooks, *The Road to Dignity, A Century of Conflict* (New York: Atheneum, 1981). The best treatment of the first major figure in the union is David Lyon, *The World of P.J. McGuire* (Ann Arbor: University Microfilms, 1972).

3. Quoted in Maxwell Raddock, *Portrait of An American Labor Leader: William L. Hutcheson* (New York: American Institute of Social Sciences, 1955), 113.

4. Brooks, *Road to Dignity*, 18-19.

5. Brooks, *Road to Dignity*, 18.

6. Brooks, *Road to Dignity*, 19.

7. Brooks, *Road to Dignity*, 22.

8. Triplett, "Oregon Labor Movement," 1-10.

9. *Carpenter* 3, September 1883, 5.

10. *Carpenter* 3, October 1883, 3.

11. *Carpenter* 4, February 1884, 3.

12. *Carpenter* 4, February 1884, 3.

13. *Carpenter* 3, November 1883, 5.

14. *Carpenter* 3, November 1883, 5.

15. *Carpenter* 3, November 1883, 5.

16. *Carpenter* 4, February 1884, 5.

17. *Carpenter* 4, April 1884, 5.

18. *Carpenter* 4, May 1884, 5.

19. *Carpenter* 4, June 1884, 3.

20. *Carpenter* 4, May 1884, 5.

21. *Carpenter* 4, May 1884, 5.

22. *Carpenter* 4, May 1884, 5.
23. *Carpenter* 4, July 1884, 3.
24. *Carpenter* 4, July 1884, 3.
25. *Carpenter* 5, April 1885, 5.
26. *Carpenter* 7, August 1887, 2.
27. Triplett, "Oregon Labor Movement," 28. The AFL itself was said to have been reborn in 1886, after a shaky start in 1881.
28. Triplett, "Oregon Labor Movement," 28.
29. *Carpenter* 9, May 1889, 1.
30. Triplett, "Oregon Labor Movement," 38.

CHAPTER TWO   "Eight Hours Will Constitute . . ."

1. John Morton Blum et al., *The National Experience*, vol. 2 (5th ed., New York: Harcourt Brace Jovanovich, 1981), 469.
2. Walter Galenson, *The United Brotherhood of Carpenters, the First Hundred Years* (Cambridge: Harvard University Press, 1983), 43-45; Thomas Brooks, *The Road to Dignity, A Century of Conflict* (New York: Atheneum, 1981), 38.
3. *See* John G. Cawelti, *Apostles of the Self-Made Man* (Chicago: University of Chicago Press, 1965), for a discussion of the self-made man.
4. Brooks, *Road to Dignity*, 37-38.
5. *Oregonian*, 3 September 1889.
6. *Oregonian*, 3 September 1889.
7. Jack Triplett, "History of the Oregon Labor Movement Prior to the New Deal" (Master's thesis, University of California, Berkeley, 1961), 32-33. *See also* the *Oregonian*, 15 May and 9 July 1889.
8. Triplett, "Oregon Labor Movement," 33.
9. *Oregonian*, 23 March 1890.
10. *Carpenter* 10, 15 March 1890, 1.
11. *Oregonian*, 23 March and 30 April 1890.
12. *Oregonian*, 23 March and 30 April 1890.
13. Triplett, "Oregon Labor Movement," 33.
14. *Oregonian*, 30 April 1890.
15. *Oregonian*, 30 April 1890.
16. *Oregonian*, 30 April 1890.
17. *Oregonian*, 1 May 1890.
18. *Oregonian*, 2 May 1890.
19. *Oregonian*, 2 May 1890. Pennoyer was reading the strength of the reform trend in Oregon politics and attempting to harness his political fortunes to it (as it happened, successfully). *See* Dorothy O. Johansen and Charles M.

Gates, *Empire of the Columbia* (New York, Harper & Row, 1967), 357.
20. *Oregonian*, 2 May 1890.
21. *Oregonian*, 11 May 1890.
22. *Oregonian*, 11 May 1890.
23. *Oregonian*, 11 May 1890.
24. *Oregonian*, 11 May 1890.

CHAPTER THREE   Era of Confrontation

1. Jack Triplett, "History of the Oregon Labor Movement Prior to the New Deal" (Master's thesis, University of California, Berkeley, 1961), 41; and Omar Hoskins, "Some Aspects of Oregon Labor Organization from 1853 to 1902" (Bachelor's thesis, Reed College, 1935), 73.
2. E. Kimbark MacColl, *The Shaping of a City: Business and Politics in Portland, Oregon, 1885-1915* (Portland: The Georgian Press, 1976), 105.
3. Carl Degler, *Out of the Past* (New York: Harper & Row, 1970), 424. *See also* Dorothy O. Johansen and Charles M. Gates, *Empire of the Columbia* (New York: Harper & Row, 1967), 360-65, for a summary of the regional impact of the depression of 1893; and MacColl, *Shaping of a City*, 99, 100-106, for the impact on Portland.
4. MacColl, *Shaping of a City*, 105.
5. Triplett, "Oregon Labor Movement," 41.
6. Triplett, "Oregon Labor Movement," 41-42, provides a good summary of the relationship between the Federated Trades Association and the Central Labor Council. *See also* the *Oregonian*, 24 July 1983.
7. *Portland Labor Press*, 11 September 1902. By this date, Local No. 50 had been meeting in the Eagle's Hall, at Second and Yamhill streets, for two years.
8. *Portland Labor Press*, 25 June 1902.
9. *Portland Labor Press*, 18 September 1902. The union told the city council it would stand the cost of an injunction to prevent construction in Vancouver.
10. *Portland Labor Press*, 16 October 1902.
11. Kelly Loe, ed., *Convention Proceedings of the Oregon State Federation of Labor for the Years 1902, 1903, 1904, 1905, 1907* (Portland: Oregon State Federation of Labor, 1928), 1.
12. Loe, *Convention Proceedings*, 1.
13. Progressivism is discussed in detail in Richard Hofstadter, *Age of Reform* (New York: Vintage Books, 1955); and Eric Goldman, *Rendezvous With Destiny, A History of Modern American Reform* (New York: Vintage Books, 1977).
14. Loe, *Convention Proceedings*, 2.
15. *See* Alexander Saxton, *Indispensable Enemy: Labor and the Anti-Chinese Move-*

ment in California (Berkeley: University of California Press, 1971), for a thorough discussion of anti-Asian sentiment in California, which can be generalized to the entire West Coast. In Gordon B. Dodds, *Oregon: A History* (New York: W.W. Norton, 1977), the author notes anti-Chinese sentiment as early as 1869 at Oregon City, where an anti-Chinese labor group, the White Laborers' Association, sprang up. *See 77.*

16. Carlos Schwantes, "Protest in a Promised Land: Unemployment, Disinheritance, and the Origin of Labor Militancy in the Pacific Northwest, 1885-1886," *Western Historical Quarterly* 13, October 1982, 373-90, takes the view that the anti-Chinese crusades primarily catalyzed labor organization in the Northwest for unemployed white workers.

17. *Oregon Journal*, 20 May 1902.

18. *Oregon Journal*, 29 May 1902. *See also Journal* editorial, 21 May 1902.

19. *Oregon Journal*, 29 May 1902. *See also Portland Labor Press*, 29 May 1902.

20. *Portland Labor Press*, 29 May 1902. *See also Oregonian*, 23 and 24 May 1902.

21. *Portland Labor Press*, 29 May 1902. *See also Oregonian*, 30 May 1902.

22. *Oregonian*, 6 June 1902.

23. *Portland Labor Press*, 3 July 1902.

24. *Portland Labor Press*, 19 March 1903.

25. *Oregonian*, 2, 3 and 4 April 1903.

26. *Oregonian*, 3 April 1903.

27. *Oregonian*, 2, 3 and 4 April 1902.

28. *Oregonian*, 3 April 1903.

29. *Oregonian*, 3 April 1903.

30. *Oregonian*, 3 April 1903.

31. *Oregonian*, 9 May 1903.

32. Triplett, "Oregon Labor Movement," 45.

33. *Oregonian*, 9 May 1903. The *Labor Press* flatly contradicted the *Oregonian*'s account, but the latter was correct. *See Portland Labor Press*, 15 May 1903.

34. Robert W. Rydell, *All the World's a Fair*, (Ph.D. dissertation, University of California, Los Angeles, 1982); *see* Ch. 5 for a good overview of the social, political and economic context in which the fair was held. *See also Portland Labor Press*, 24 February and 3 March 1905.

35. *Portland Labor Press*, 10 March and 27 May 1905. *See also* note in *Carpenter* 14, November 1904, 9; and *Carpenter* 25, February 1905, 1.

36. *See Portland Labor Press*, 24 July 1903; and the *Oregonian*, 28 and 29 March 1903.

37. *Portland Labor Press*, 1 January 1904.

38. *Portland Labor Press*, 23 October 1903.

39. *Portland Labor Press*, 23 October 1903.

40. *Portland Labor Press*, 20 November 1904.

CHAPTER FOUR   Making Adjustments

1. *Portland Labor Press*, 9 February 1906.
2. *Portland Labor Press*, 9 February 1906.
3. *Portland Labor Press*, 9 February 1906.
4. *Portland Labor Press*, 6 June 1906.
5. *Portland Labor Press*, 4 May 1906. An article by R.A. Harris in the *Oregonian* of 29 April 1907, entitled "Status of Labor Unions in Portland," paints a similarly rosy picture.
6. *Portland Labor Press*, 23 June 1908.
7. *Portland Labor Press*, 30 June 1908.
8. *Portland Labor Press*, 1 September 1908.
9. *Portland Labor Press*, 29 April 1909.
10. *Portland Labor Press*, 16 December 1909.
11. *Portland Labor Press*, 20 January 1910.
12. *Portland Labor Press*, 20 January 1910.
13. *Portland Labor Press*, 16 September 1909.
14. *Portland Labor Press*, 16 December 1909.
15. *Portland Labor Press*, 16 December 1909.
16. *Portland Labor Press*, 7 October 1909.
17. *Portland Labor Press*, 28 October 1909.
18. E. Kimbark MacColl, *The Shaping of a City: Business and Politics in Portland, Oregon, 1885-1915* (Portland: The Georgian Press, 1976), 489.
19. *Oregon Labor Press*, 19 January 1911.
20. *Oregon Labor Press*, 19 January 1911. Figures for wages in other occupations and local prices are from Joseph Gaston, *Portland: Its History and Builders*, vol. 1, 629 and MacColl, *Shaping of a City*, 489.
21. *Oregon Labor Press*, 3 August 1911.
22. *Oregon Labor Press*, 2 February 1911.
23. *Oregon Labor Press*, 2 February 1911.

CHAPTER FIVE   The Problems of War and Peace

1. Throughout 1909 and 1910, the *Carpenter* was replete with pleas from the Portland locals that carpenters stay away from the city. The notices said outlanders were being duped by unscrupulous real-estate promoters and open-shop advocates wishing to flood the labor market with unemployed (and, therefore, desperate) men. *See* the *Carpenter* 28, December 1908, 45; 29,

April 1909, 41; 29, July 1909, 42.

2. The *Oregonian* also began to editorialize strongly against organized labor as problems of equity faded from debate and more complex matters began to dominate labor's agenda. On these issues, such as lawful boycotts, and the editor's perception of labor's drift toward socialism, the newspaper gave the unions no quarter. *See* editorials in the *Oregonian*, 6 April 1908 and 4 March 1909.

3. George Ankeny, "Local No. 583," in *Oregon Carpenters' Yearbook*, Portland: Oregon State Council of Carpenters, 1962, 77.

4. *See* Appendix 11.

5. *See* Appendix 11. *See also* "Carpenters Local No. 1020 Honors Old Time Members," *Oregon Carpenters' Yearbook*, 1964, 8. This indicates that No. 1020 originated in 1901 as shipwrights', caulkers', and shipjoiners' Local No. 1, at that time affiliated with the Pacific Coast Maritime Builders Association.

6. Although figures are unavailable, evidence suggests that the shipwrights maintained membership in a ratio of about 1:7 to the two large locals. Moreover, in later years, particularly during the two world wars, carpenters from the other locals took work in the shipyards, thus undermining No. 1020's position.

7. Ankeny, "Local No. 583," 77.

8. Ankeny, "Local No. 583," 77.

9. *Portland Labor Press*, 14 August 1915.

10. *Portland Labor Press*, 2 October 1915.

11. *Portland Labor Press*, 2 October 1915.

12. Jack Triplett, "History of the Oregon Labor Movement Prior to the New Deal" (Master's thesis, University of California, Berkeley, 1961), 100.

13. Triplett, "Oregon Labor Movement," 100.

14. *Oregon Labor Press*, 12 February 1916. With the issue of 4 September 1915, the *Portland Labor Press* became the *Oregon Labor Press*, hereinafter so cited.

15. Dean Collins, *Stars of Oregon* (Portland: Binford & Mort, 1943), 101.

16. Collins, *Stars of Oregon*, 101.

17. *Oregon Labor Press*, 1 September 1917.

18. *Oregon Labor Press*, 1 September 1917. *See also* Harold Hyman, *Soldiers and Spruce: Origins of the Loyal Legions of Loggers and Lumbermen* (Berkeley and Los Angeles: University of California, Los Angeles Press, 1963), for an account of organized labor in the lumber industry in World War 1.

19. Lancaster Pollard, "The Pacific Northwest: A Regional Study," *Oregon Historical Quarterly* 52, December 1951, pp. 211-34. *See also* Collins, *Stars of Oregon*, 101.

20. Collins, *Stars of Oregon*, 103.

21. *Oregon Labor Press*, 29 September 1917.

22. *Oregon Labor Press*, 16 February 1918.
23. *Oregon Labor Press*, 16 February 1918.
24. *Oregon Labor Press*, 14 September 1918.
25. Emergency Fleet Corporation, *Shipyard Occupations* (Philadelphia: U.S. Shipping Board, 1918), 125.
26. Emergency Fleet Corporation, *Shipyard Occupations*, 125.
27. Emergency Fleet Corporation, *Shipyard Occupations*, 107.
28. Emergency Fleet Corporation, *Shipyard Occupations*, 107.
29. Emergency Fleet Corporation, *Shipyard Occupations*, 128.
30. Emergency Fleet Corporation, *Shipyard Occupations*, 113.
31. Emergency Fleet Corporation, *Shipyard Occupations*, 113.
32. Emergency Fleet Corporation, *Shipyard Occupations*, 127.
33. Emergency Fleet Corporation, *Shipyard Occupations*, 129.
34. Emergency Fleet Corporation, *Shipyard Occupations*, 83.
35. *Oregon Labor Press*, 16 February 1918.
36. Emergency Fleet Corporation, *Yearbook* (U.S. Shipping Board, 1919), 32, Oregon Historical Society files.
37. Emergency Fleet Corporation, *Yearbook*, 8.
38. *Oregon Labor Press*, 14 September 1918.
39. *See* Maxwell Raddock, *Portrait of a Labor Leader: William L. Hutcheson* (New York: American Institute of Social Sciences, 1955), pp. 80-108, for an examination of this problem, and Walter Galenson, *The United Brotherhood of Carpenters: The First Hundred Years* (Cambridge, Harvard University Press, 1983), pp. 184-92.
40. A strike scheduled for 30 December 1916 at the Northwest Steel Company had been thwarted when the owner closed the yard "for repairs."
41. *Oregon Labor Press*, 18 August 1917.
42. *Oregon Labor Press*, 18 August 1917.
43. *See Oregon Labor Press*, 6, 13 and 20 January 1917. The closed shop refers to the practice of hiring only union members. The open shop, its opposite, allows nonunion workers to be hired.
44. *Oregon Labor Press*, 8 September 1917.
45. *Oregon Labor Press*, 15 September 1917.
46. *Oregon Labor Press*, 15 September 1917.
47. *Oregon Labor Press*, 22 September 1917.
48. *Oregon Labor Press*, 22 September 1917.
49. *Oregon Labor Press*, 29 September 1917.
50. *Oregon Labor Press*, 27 October 1917.
51. *Oregon Labor Press*, 27 October 1917.
52. *Oregon Labor Press*, 23 February 1918.
53. *Oregon Labor Press*, 23 February 1918.

54. *Oregon Labor Press*, 2 November 1918.
55. *Oregon Labor Press*, 25 November 1918.
56. *Oregon Labor Press*, 2 February 1918.
57. *Oregon Labor Press*, 21 December 1918.
58. *Oregon Labor Press*, 16 November 1918.
59. Triplett, "Oregon Labor Movement," 124. The *Labor Press* carried complete transcripts of testimony for the duration of the hearings of the Board.
60. Triplett, "Oregon Labor Movement," 124.
61. Collins, *Stars of Oregon*, 105.
62. *Oregon Labor Press*, 21 February 1920.
63. *Oregon Labor Press*, 2 February 1917.

CHAPTER SIX   Breathing Room

1. *Oregon Labor Press*, 10 January 1920. It should be noted that the *Labor Press* steadfastly and consistently resisted the antiradical hysteria of the day.
2. Harry Carlson, retired carpenter, former trustee and financial secretary of Local No. 583, and Dudley Franco, retired millman of Local No. 1746, president, Portland Council of Carpenters, joint interview, 9 February 1983.
3. Carlson-Franco interview, 9 February 1983.
4. *Oregon Labor Press*, 15 May 1920.
5. *Oregon Labor Press*, 7 February 1920.
6. *Oregon Labor Press*, 7 February 1920.
7. Discussions of the "American Plan" and its impact on the carpenters are found in Walter Galenson, *The United Brotherhood of Carpenters, The First Hundred Years* (Cambridge: Harvard University Press, 1983), pp. 201-206; and in Thomas Brooks, *The Road to Dignity, A Century of Conflict* (New York: Atheneum, 1981), pp. 118-22. The origins and significance of the American Plan to organize labor in general is covered successfully in James R. Green, *The World of the Worker: Labor in Twentieth Century America* (New York: Hill and Wang, 1980), pp. 119-20.
8. *Oregon Labor Press*, 4 September 1920.
9. Andrew Sears, retired carpenter, Local No. 226, interview, 17 September 1981; and Carlson-Franco interview.
10. Association for Building and Construction, Minutes, 17 October 1922, Local No. 247, files.
11. Sears interview.
12. Sears interview.
13. Association for Building and Construction, Minutes, 25 November 1922, Local No. 247, files.

14. *Oregon Labor Press*, 25 February 1927.
15. *Oregon Labor Press*, 25 February 1927; Sears interview.
16. *Oregon Labor Press*, 1 January 1926.
17. *Oregon Labor Press*, 12 February 1926.
18. Interview with Clarence Blakeley, retired carpenter, former member Klamath Falls Local No. 190, 28 June 1983. This observation was confirmed in the Carlson-Franco interview.
19. *See Oregon Labor Press* for 1926, especially 15 January, 12 and 19 February, 19 March, 16 July, and 26 November. This was the beginning of association bargaining by both labor and management, a tactic discussed in detail in Chapter 7.
20. *Oregon Labor Press*, 13 July, 21 September, and 28 December 1928, and 4 January 1929, for wages and detail on the evolution of the five-day week. Detail on journeyman hours also in Sears interview.
21. *Oregon Labor Press*, 16 July 1926.
22. *Oregon Labor Press*, 16 July 1926.
23. *Oregon Labor Press*, 3 January 1920.
24. Sears interview, corroborated in Carlson-Franco interview.
25. Sears interview, corroborated in Carlson-Franco interview.
26. Sears interview, corroborated in Carlson-Franco interview.
27. On the subject of Douglas fir and its marketing, *see*, e.g., Ralph W. Hidy et al., *Timber and Men: The Weyerhaeuser Story* (New York: Macmillan Co., 1963), William B. Greeley, *Forests and Men* (New York: Doubleday, 1951); and Ellis Lucia, *Headrig: The Story of the West Coast Lumber Industry* (Portland: Overland West Press, 1965).
28. Interview with Dudley Franco, 4 March 1983.
29. Franco interview, corroborated by Carlson and Sears interviews.
30. Blakeley interview.
31. Franco interview.

CHAPTER SEVEN   Depression and War

1. *Oregon Labor Press*, 20 June 1930.
2. Interview with Art Wickstrand, retired carpenter, former trustee, Local No. 226, and business agent, 17 September 1981.
3. *See* E. Kimbark MacColl, *The Growth of a City: Power and Politics in Portland, Oregon, 1915-1950* (Portland: The Georgian Press, 1979), esp. pp. 490, 492-93. *See also* John Tess, *Uphill, Downhill, Yamhill: The Evolution of the Yamhill Historic District in Portland, Oregon* (Portland: Bureau of Planning, 1977), pp. 30-34; *Oregon Labor Press*, 23 June and 12 December 1933; *Oregonian*, 14 De-

cember 1933; and *Oregon Journal*, 26 December 1968.

4. MacColl, *Growth of a City*, pp. 454-55. *See also Oregon Labor Press*, 7 and 31 March and 21 April 1933.

5. *Oregon Labor Press*, 7 March 1933.

6. *Oregon Labor Press*, 14 July 1933.

7. Henry Steele Commager, ed., *Documents of American History*, vol. 2 (Englewood Cliffs: Prentice-Hall, 1973), 273.

8. Maggie Doran, *Building the Oregon Country* (Portland: Associated General Contractors, 1980), 123. *See also* Dorothy O. Johansen and Charles M. Gates, *Empire of the Columbia* (New York; Harper & Row, 1967), Ch. 31, for a concise background to the damming of the Columbia River. E. Kimbark MacColl, *The Shaping of a City: Business and Politics in Portland, Oregon, 1885-1915* (Portland: The Georgian Press, 1976), pp. 436-48, discusses the political and economic implications of the dam's construction for Portland.

9. Carlson-Franco interview.

10. Interview with Harry Carlson, 22 February 1983.

11. *See* Walter Galenson, *The United Brotherhood of Carpenters, The First Hundred Years* (Cambridge: Harvard University Press, 1983), 254-56. *See also* James R. Green, *The World of the Worker: Labor in Twentieth Century America* (New York: Hill and Wang, 1980), 151-52.

12. Maxwell Raddock, *Portrait of a Labor Leader: William L. Hutcheson* (New York: American Institute of Social Sciences, 1955), 201. *See also* Galenson, *United Brotherhood of Carpenters*, Ch. 11; and Green, *World of the Worker*, particularly 152-53.

13. Galenson, *United Brotherhood of Carpenters*, 252-53. Galenson provides the most satisfying documentation of the brotherhood's involvement with the CIO in the Pacific Northwest. His research is summarized here insofar as it is relevant to the Portland carpenters.

14. Franco interview.

15. Franco interview.

16. Franco interview.

17. *See* Green, *World of the Worker*, 224; and Galenson, *United Brotherhood of Carpenters*, 308-9, for background. When the brotherhood refused to satisfy the preliminary agreement between the two organizations, the AFL retaliated by barring the union from its deliberations. The brotherhood responded by walking out of AFL councils. When the AFL and CIO merger was completed, the brotherhood remained, at best, lukewarm to it.

18. *Oregon Labor Press*, 3 April 1936.

19. William E. Leuchtenberg, *Franklin D. Roosevelt and the New Deal* (New York: Harper & Row, 1963), 194-95.

20. Carl Abbott, *Portland: Planning, Politics, and Growth in a Twentieth Century*

(Lincoln: University of Nebraska Press, 1983), 131-32; and MacColl, *Growth of a City*, 593-96. *See also Oregon Labor Press*, 23 September and 4 November 1938.

21. *Oregon Labor Press*, 24 November 1939.
22. *Oregon Labor Press*, 5 January 1940.
23. *Oregon Labor Press*, 5 January 1940.
24. *Oregon Labor Press*, 5 January 1940.
25. *Oregon Labor Press*, 19 July 1940.
26. *Oregon Labor Press*, 25 August 1939.
27. *Oregon Labor Press*, 25 August 1939.
28. *Oregon Labor Press*, 12 December 1941.
29. *Oregon Labor Press*, 12 December 1941.
30. *Oregon Labor Press*, 18 October 1940.
31. *Oregon Labor Press*, 5 September 1941.
32. *Oregon Labor Press*, 5 September 1941.
33. *Oregon Labor Press*, 24 January 1981.
34. There is general agreement among historians that World War II was the key to finally overcoming the economic malaise of the thirties. *See* John Morton Blum, *V Was For Victory: Politics and American Culture During World War II* (New York: Harcourt Brace Jovanovich, 1976), 9, for background. Leuchtenberg, *Franklin D. Roosevelt*, 318-19, focuses concisely on the issue in the context of the 1940 presidential campaign.
35. MacColl, *Growth of a City*, 571.
36. MacColl, *Growth of a City*, 571-73. A full account of Kaiser's shipbuilding success in Portland and its relationship to the entire maritime war effort is offered in Frederic C. Lane et al., *Ships for Victory: A History of Shipbuilding Under the United States Maritime Commission in World War II* (Baltimore: Johns Hopkins Press, 1951). *See also A Survey of Shipyard Operations in the Portland, Oregon Metropolitan Area*, (Washington, D.C.: U.S. War Manpower Commission, 1943).
37. *Survey of Shipyard Operations*, 8.
38. *Survey of Shipyard Operations*, 8.
39. *Survey of Shipyard Operations*, 8.
40. *Survey of Shipyard Operations*, 8. *See also* MacColl, *Growth of a City*, 573-75, for background on Harvey Dick, owner of a machine shop, where an innovation in the casting of stern frames enabled him to turn them out at a rate of one a day, thereby saving much idle time on each ship. Details from interview with Joe Stanley, retired marine carpenter, former member of Local No. 1020, 10 June 1983.
41. Stanley interview. Statistics in *Ship Construction, Eight Selected West Coast Yards, 1941-1945*, (Washington, D.C.: War Manpower Commission, n.d.), 2.
42. Stanley interview.

43.   Stanley interview. Also interview with George Edwards, carpenter, former shipyard worker, secretary of Local No. 247, 30 July 1983. *Survey of Shipyard Operations*, 8.

44.   Edwards interview.

45.   Stanley interview.

46.   Lane et al., *Ships for Victory*, 77.

47.   Lane et al., *Ships for Victory*, 280. The shipyard wage was lower than journeyman wages in the civilian sector. *See* Appendix 1 for Portland carpenters' wages during the war years.

48.   Carlson-Franco interview.

49.   Carlson-Franco interview. Sleeman was proud of the relationship he had cultivated with both Henry Kaiser and his son, Edgar. The fine relations between labor and management on Kaiser projects since then, Sleeman said, were "just a question of men having confidence in each other." Quoted from *Oregon Carpenters' Yearbook* (Portland: Oregon State Council of Carpenters, 1962), 77.

50.   Lane et al., *Ships for Victory*, 241. The thirteen unions were those of the blacksmiths, boilermakers, electrical workers, operating engineers, laborers, metal polishers, machinists, pattern makers, molders, plumbers and steamfitters, sheet-metal workers, carpenters, and painters.

51.   Lane et al., *Ships for Victory*, 248.

52.   Lane et al., *Ships for Victory*, 248.

53.   Carlson-Franco interview. It should be noted that Kaiser recruited in major cities across the nation for work in his Portland yards. *See* Lane et al., *Ships for Victory*, 248.

54.   Carlson-Franco interview.

55.   Carlson-Franco interview.

56.   Carlson-Franco interview. *See also* Lane et al., *Ships for Victory*, 254.

57.   *Oregon Labor Press*, 3 September 1943.

58.   *Oregon Labor Press*, 3 November 1944.

59.   *Oregon Labor Press*, 17 March and 28 April, 1944.

CHAPTER EIGHT   The Postwar Era

1.   U.S. Bureau of the Census, *Statistical Abstract of the United States*, 103rd ed. (Washington, D.C., 1980).

2.   U.S. Bureau of the Census, *Historical Statistics of the United States, Colonial Times to 1970*, Bicentennial ed. (Washington, D.C., 1975).

3.   Bureau of Census, *Historical Statistics*, 1975.

4.   Bureau of Census, *Historical Statistics*, 1975.

5. *See* Richard O. Davies, *The Age of Asphalt: The Automobile, The Freeway, and The Condition of Metropolitan America* (Philadelphia: J.B. Lippincott, 1975), p. 23 passim, for a discussion of the impact of freeway construction on the American economy and society.

6. Irving Bernstein, "Trade Union Characteristics, Membership, and Influence," *Monthly Labor Review* 82 (May 1959), 530.

7. Walter Galenson, *The United Brotherhood of Carpenters, The First Hundred Years* (Cambridge: Harvard University Press, 1983), 300-301.

8. *See* Carl Abbott, *Portland: Planning, Polictics, and Growth in a Twentieth Century City* (Lincoln: University of Nebraska Press, 1983), ch. 7, and E. Kimbark MacColl, *The Growth of a City: Power and Politics in Portland, Oregon, 1915-1950* (Portland: The Georgian Press, 1979), chs. 18-20, for discussions of Portland's economic growth and development in the immediate postwar period. *See also* "When Figures Lie," *Business Week*, 25 January 1947, 32-34, for a brief sketch of Portland's economic posture at the close of hostilities.

9. "When Figures Lie," 32-33.

10. "When Figures Lie," 32.

11. Maggie Doran, *Building the Oregon Country* (Portland: Associated General Contractors, 1980), 19.

12. Doran, *Oregon Country*, 19.

13. *See* Abbott, *Portland*, 255-57, for a discussion of the politics of the Mt. Hood decision. The *Oregon Labor Press* carried editorials on the question throughout early 1975, e.g., 24 January, 17 February, 21 March.

14. Doran, *Oregon Country*, 140.

15. Doran, *Oregon Country*, 140.

16. Figures supplied by Tri-Met, Office of Public Information, 16 October 1984.

17. Tri-Met, Office of Public Information, 16 October 1984.

18. Background to the Lloyd Center development is provided in MacColl, *Growth of a City*, 325-40, and Abbott, *Portland*, 186 and 210.

19. Interview with Roy Coles, former executive secretary, State District Council of Carpenters, 19 July 1984. *See also* the conclusions of Philip Taft, "A Labor Historian Views Changes in the Trade Union Movement," *Monthly Labor Review* 92, September 1969, 8-11, especially 8. Clark Kerr, "West Coast Labor: Its Past and Its Prospects," *Monthly Labor Review* 82, May 1959, 489-91; and, in the same issue, Arthur M. Ross, "Major Trends in Labor Relations," show how overall trends in West Coast labor relations led to this conclusion. Economic growth in the Pacific Northwest in the postwar period is discussed in Miner H. Baker, "Economic Growth Patterns in Washington and Oregon," *Monthly Labor Review* 82, May 1959, 502-8.

20. Kerr, "West Coast Labor," 490-91.

21. Coles interview. *See also* Taft, "Changes in the Trade Union Movement," for

corroboration, as well as Irving Bernstein, "Trade Union Characteristics, Membership, and Influence," *Monthly Labor Review* 82, May 1959, 530.

22. Joe Lane to Leo Larsen, 15 April 1983, Local No. 247, files.

23. Lane to Larsen, 15 April 1983.

24. Frank C. Pierson, "Building-Trades Bargaining Plan in Southern California," *Monthly Labor Review* 70, January 1950, 14.

25. *See* Appendix I. The percentage increase in wages, obviously, is not adjusted for inflation. Nevertheless, the rise in pay is significant.

26. *See* Pierson, "Building-Trades Bargaining Plan," 17-18. *See also* Van Dusen Kennedy, "Association Bargaining," *Monthly Labor Review* 82, May 1959, 541-42, for a fuller discussion of the implications of association bargaining than Pierson's.

27. These conclusions are corroborated on the local level by the interview with Mark Furman, task force representative, United Brotherhood of Carpenters, 23 August 1984, and with Coles.

28. *Oregonian*, 4 May 1983.

29. *Oregonian*, 4 May 1983.

30. *Oregonian*, 4 May 1983.

31. Galenson, *United Brotherhood of Carpenters*, 381.

32. Galenson, *United Brotherhood of Carpenters*, 381.

33. Author's notes, Local No. 247 picketing meeting, 25 March 1983.

34. Author's notes, Local No. 247 picketing meeting, 25 March 1983. *See also Oregonian*, 12 July 1982, and Galenson, *United Brotherhood of Carpenters*, 380-84. Hatch was a particularly painful case for the union because the company was one of the most prominent and active companies in Oregon, winning far more than its share of contracts.

35. *Oregonian*, 24 October 1983.

36. *Oregonian*, 24 October 1983.

37. *Oregonian*, 24 October 1983.

38. *Oregonian*, 26 July 1983. Interview with George Carbone, consul for Italy, Maritime Affairs Authority, 6 September 1984.

39. Interview with Ed Olsen, former president of Local No. 583, retired shipyard and general construction carpenter, 12 May 1983.

40. *Oregon Labor Press*, 21 September 1983. As if to confirm the industry's prognosis, Northwest Marine Iron Works was sold in mid-1984 to outside investors in order to avoid bankruptcy. It was also reported in 1984 that Northwest Marine and Dillingham Ship Repair, the two struck yards of 1983, had lost a significant contract to Japanese yards operating under government subsidy. The Port of Portland drydock was said to have suffered a loss of three hundred thousand dollars in 1983. See *Oregonian*, 16 October 1984.

41. "Recent Developments in Apprenticeship," Monthly Labor Review 69, Au-

gust 1949, 126.

42. "Recent Developments," Monthly Labor Review 69, 129.

43. "Recent Developments," Monthly Labor Review 69, 126.

44. "Recent Developments," Monthly Labor Review 69, 126.

45. Oregon Labor Press, 27 January 1950.

46. Oregon Labor Press, 13 January 1950.

47. Oregon Labor Press, 13 January 1950. For details concerning the apprenticeship trust, see "Carpenters' Master Labor Agreement," between Oregon-Columbia Chapter, the Associated General Contractors of America, Inc., and the Oregon State District Council of the UBCJA (1 June 1988-31 May 1991), 47.

48. Oregon Labor Press, 26 May 1950.

49. Oregon Labor Press, 26 January 1951.

50. Oregon Labor Press, 26 January 1951.

51. Oregon Labor Press, 2 March 1951.

52. Oregon Labor Press, 2 March 1951.

53. Oregon Labor Press, 4 September 1951.

54. Oregon Labor Press, 24 June 1959. A similar story appeared also in the Oregon Journal, 19 July 1959.

55. Oregon Labor Press, 24 June 1959; Oregon Journal, 19 July 1959.

56. Karl Krutsinger, "Apprentice Training Is Reported Lacking," in Oregon Carpenters' Yearbook (Portland: 1963), 59.

57. Krutsinger, "Apprentice Training," 59.

58. Krutsinger, "Apprentice Training," 59.

59. Krutsinger, "Apprentice Training," 59.

60. Oregon Labor Press, 18 March 1966.

61. Oregon Labor Press, 27 September 1965.

62. Oregon Labor Press, 27 September 1965.

63. For background, see Jim F. Heath, Decade of Disillusionment (Bloomington: University of Indiana Press, 1975), 117, 171, 173, 213-14, 216, 256-57, 292; Richard Polenberg, One Nation Divisible: Race, Class and Ethnicity in the United States Since 1938 (New York: Penguin Books, 1980), 7, 9; and James R. Green, The World of the Worker: Labor in Twentieth Century America (New York: Hill and Wang, 1980), especially Ch. 7.

64. Galenson, United Brotherhood of Carpenters, 345.

65. Galenson, United Brotherhood of Carpenters, 346.

66. Galenson, United Brotherhood of Carpenters, 346.

67. William A. Little and James E. Weiss, eds., Blacks in Oregon: A Statistical and Historical Report (Portland: Black Studies Center and the Center for Population Research and Census, Portland State University, 1978), 124.

68. Little and Weiss, Blacks in Oregon, 128. It is impossible to report accurately the numbers of members of minority groups belonging to the United Broth-

erhood of Carpenters as a whole or to locals, as the general office never kept such records. *See* Galenson, *United Brotherhood of Carpenters*, 346. The Portland locals have never kept such records of their own accord, either. In 1963, the No. 226 newsletter observed: "Some time ago the General Office inquired into the number of Negros [sic] who are members but have no way of knowing how many. Further, it was stated that we have never recorded the race, color or creed of our members. . . . A member is recognized only as a brother. 226 asks but one thing of a member—that he conduct himself as a gentleman." (From *226 Reporter*, 11 October 1963.)

Elizabeth McLagan, *A Peculiar Paradise: A History of Blacks in Oregon*, 1788-1940 (Portland: The Georgian Press, 1980), provides further background on blacks and their occupations in Portland. Also refer to "Report on the Negro in Portland: A Progress Report, 1945-1957," *Portland City Club Bulletin* 37, 19 April 1957, 355-70, for a view of social and economic conditions among Portland's black population in the postwar era.

69. *Oregon Labor Press*, 10 May 1967; *see also* 19 July 1968 and 6 September 1968.
70. *Oregon Labor Press*, 7 February 1969.
71. Interview with Kate Barrett, trustee of Local No. 247, 20 September 1984.
72. Barrett interview.
73. Barrett interview.
74. Galenson, *United Brotherhood of Carpenters*, 381.
75. Coles interview.
76. Figures from Homebuilders Association of Portland Office of Public Affairs, 16 October 1984.
77. Interview with Fred I. Weber, Jr., economist, Homebuilders Association of Portland, 18 September 1984.
78. Weber interview.
79. Weber interview.
80. Weber interview. Corroborated by Coles and Furman interviews.
81. Weber interview.
82. "Structure of the Residential Building Industry, 1949," *Monthly Labor Review* 73, October 1951, 456.
83. "Residential Building Industry," *Monthly Labor Review* 73, 456.
84. Furman and Weber interviews.
85. Furman and Weber interviews.
86. Furman interview.
87. Furman and Coles interviews.
88. Furman interview.
89. *Oregonian*, 12 February 1982.
90. Weber interview.
91. Weber interview.

92.   Weber interview.
93.   Weber interview.

EPILOGUE

 1.   David Johnson to author, 6 April 1983.
 2.   *Oregon Labor Press*, 21 October 1983.
 3.   *Oregon Labor Press*, 21 October 1983.
 4.   In 1984, the marine carpenters split from No. 247 to form a separate local, No. 611.
 5.   *Oregonian*, 2 July 1982.
 6.   *Oregonian*, 2 July 1982.
 7.   *Oregonian*, 2 July 1982.
 8.   *Oregon Labor Press*, 21 October 1983.
 9.   *Oregon Labor Press*, 21 October 1983.
10.   *Oregon Labor Press*, 21 October 1983.
11.   *Oregon Journal*, 18 July 1982.
12.   Preliminary proposal, "Construction Industry Joint Labor-Management Cooperation Committee," 1982; "Labor Management Group Wins Federal Grant," press release from the office of the State District Council of Carpenters, Portland, Oregon. *See also Oregonian*, 24 August 1983, and *Daily Journal of Commerce*, 25 August 1983.
13.   "Construction Industry Joint Labor-Management Cooperation Committee" proposal.

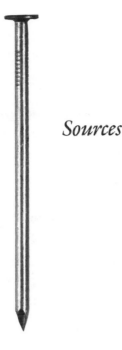

Sources

THOSE WHO STUDY THE LATE-NINETEENTH- AND twentieth-century history of Portland will find much to reward their efforts in the work of E. Kimbark MacColl and Carl Abbott. MacColl, in *The Shaping of a City: Business and Politics in Portland, Oregon, 1885-1915*, and *The Growth of a City: Power and Politics in Portland, Oregon, 1915-1950*, has provided in rich detail a study of the planting and growth of the political and economic structure of Portland. Abbott, in *Portland: Planning, Politics, and Growth in a Twentieth Century City*, has exhaustively documented and analyzed the changing physical aspect of the city over the current century. These admirable works are essential to a full understanding of the social and economic atmosphere of Portland over the last one hundred years.

Unfortunately, but understandably, neither MacColl nor Abbott is much concerned with labor in Portland's development. Their work rightly concentrates on documenting the activities of the political, economic and planning elites. Yet the role of labor was, and is, crucial to the story of Portland's development. The problem for students of labor is that nobody has undertaken the task.

This lack of research into Portland's labor history is due, no doubt, to a

149

distinct lack of materials' having been collected, either formally or informally, in the area. Part of the problem has been the reluctance of laboring men and women to commit their thoughts to paper, or to husband significant documents.

On the other hand, valuable resources are at hand to give the interested scholar a foothold in this significant field. The *Oregon Labor Press* is available on microfilm at the Oregon Historical Society and (for most of the century's issues) at Portland State University's library. Although clearly not entirely unbiased, the *Labor Press* has faithfully reported the labor community's activities for the whole century. As the official organ of Oregon's unions, it is an essential source. Jack Triplett, "The Oregon Labor Movement Prior to the New Deal," an M.A. thesis on microfilm at the Oregon Historical Society, is also a valuable tool, particularly for the late nineteenth century. The *Monthly Labor Review* at Portland State University is a mine of information on national and regional labor trends. Taped interviews with women shipyard workers during World War II, at the Oregon Historical Society, offer insights into the role of women in the workplace at a critical point in history.

These are a few of the starting places for the fuller study of Portland's labor history that needs to be undertaken. It is hoped that the following bibliography will also contribute to future research in this neglected field.

BOOKS

Abbott, Carl. *Portland: Planning, Politics, and Growth in a Twentieth Century City.* Lincoln: University of Nebraska Press, 1983.

Barbash, Jack. *American Unions: Structure, Government and Politics.* Philadelphia Book Company, 1966.

Beirne, Joseph D. *Challenges on Labor—New Rules for American Trade Unions.* Englewood Cliffs: Prentice-Hall, 1969.

Blum, John Morton. *V Was for Victory: Politics and American Culture During World War II.* New York: Harcourt Brace Jovanovich, 1976.

——— et al. *The National Experience*, vol. 2. 5th ed. New York: Harcourt Brace Jovanovich, 1981.

Brooks, Thomas. *The Road to Dignity, A Century of Conflict.* New York: Atheneum Press, 1981.

Cawelti, John G. *Apostles of the Self-Made Man*. Chicago: University of Chicago Press, 1965.

Cochran, Thomas, and William Miller. *The Age of Enterprise: A Social History of Industrial America*. New York: Harper & Row, 1961.

Collins, Dean. *Stars of Oregon*. Portland: Binford & Mort, 1943.

Commager, Henry Steele, ed. *Documents of American History*, vol. 2. Englewood Cliffs: Prentice-Hall, 1973.

Commons, John R., et al. *History of Labor in the United States*, vol. 1. New York: Macmillan Co., 1918.

Davies, Richard O. *The Age of Asphalt: The Automobile, The Freeway, and The Condition of Metropolitan America*. Philadelphia: J.B. Lippincott, 1975.

Degler, Carl. *Out of the Past*. New York: Harper & Row, 1970.

Dodds, Gordon B. *Oregon: A History*. New York: W.W. Norton, 1977.

Doran, Maggie. *Building the Oregon Country*. Portland: Associated General Contractors, 1980.

Faulkner, Harold M. *American Economic History*. 6th ed. New York: Harper & Brothers, 1949.

Foner, Philip. *A History of the Labor Movement in the United States*. 4 vols. New York: International Publishers, 1947.

Galenson, Walter. *The United Brotherhood of Carpenters, The First Hundred Years*. Cambridge: Harvard University Press, 1983.

Gaston, Joseph. *Portland: Its History and Builders*, vol. 1. Chicago: S.J. Clarke Publishing Co., 1911.

Goldman, Eric. *Rendezvous With Destiny, A History of Modern American Reform*. New York: Vintage Books, 1977.

Gompers, Samuel. *Seventy Years of Life and Labor*. 2 vols. New York: Dutton, 1957.

Greeley, William B. *Forests and Men*. New York: Doubleday, 1951.

Green, James R. *The World of the Worker: Labor in Twentieth Century America*. New York: Hill and Wang, 1980.

Gutman, Herbert. *Work, Culture and Society in Industrializing America*. New York: Alfred A. Knopf, 1976.

Harris, William H. *Keeping the Faith—A. Philip Randolph, Milton P. Webster, and the Brotherhood of Sleeping Car Porters, 1925-37*. Champagne: University of Illinois Press, 1977.

Heath, Jim F. *Decade of Disillusionment*. Bloomington: University of Indiana Press, 1975.

Hidy, Ralph W. et al. *Timber and Men: The Weyerhaeuser Story*. New York: Macmillan Co., 1963.

Hofstadter, Richard. *Age of Reform*. New York: Vintage Books, 1955.

Hyman, Harold. *Soldiers and Spruce: Origins of the Loyal Legion of Loggers and Lumbermen*. Berkeley and Los Angeles: University of California Press, Institute of Industrial Relations, 1963.

Johansen, Dorothy O., and Charles M. Gates. *Empire of the Columbia*. 2nd ed. New York: Harper & Row, 1967.

Josephson, Matthew. *The Robber Barons*. New York: Harcourt-Brace, 1934.

Lane, Frederic C. et al. *Ships for Victory: A History of Shipbuilding Under the United States Maritime Commission in World War II*. Baltimore: Johns Hopkins Press, 1951.

Leuchtenberg, William E. *Franklin D. Roosevelt and the New Deal*. New York: Harper & Row, 1963.

———. *A Troubled Feast: American Society Since 1945*. Boston: Little, Brown, 1973.

Little, William A., and James E. Weiss, eds. *Blacks in Oregon: A Statistical and Historical Report*. Portland: Black Studies Center and the Center for Population

Research and Census, Portland State University, 1978.

Lucia, Ellis. *Headrig: The Story of the West Coast Lumber Industry*. Portland: Overland West Press, 1965.

Lynd, Alice, and Staughton Lynd. *Rank and File: Personal Histories by Working Class Organizers*. Boston: Beacon Press, 1973.

Lyon, David. *The World of P.J. McGuire*. Ann Arbor: University Microfilms, 1972.

Matles, James J., and James Higgins. *Them and Us: Struggles of a Rank-and-File Union*. Englewood Cliffs: Prentice-Hall, 1974.

MacColl, E. Kimbark. *The Growth of a City: Power and Politics in Portland, Oregon, 1915-1950*. Portland: The Georgian Press, 1979.

————. *The Shaping of a City: Business and Politics in Portland, Oregon, 1885-1915*. Portland: The Georgian Press, 1976.

McLagan, Elizabeth. *A Peculiar Paradise: A History of Blacks in Oregon, 1788-1940*. Portland: The Georgian Press, 1980.

Meier, August, and Elliot Rudivick. *Black Detroit and the Rise of the Union*. New York: Oxford University Press, 1979.

Pelz, Ruth, and Nigel Adams. *Organize: A Labor History Curriculum for Washington State*. Olympia, State of Washington: Division of Instructional Programs and Services, 1983.

Polenberg, Richard. *One Nation Divisible: Race, Class and Ethnicity in the United States Since 1938*. New York: Penguin Books, 1980.

Raddock, Maxwell. *Portrait of an American Labor Leader: William L. Hutcheson*. New York: American Institute of Social Sciences, 1955.

Rutner, Sidney, James Soltow and Richard Sylla. *The Evolution of the American Economy*. New York: Basic Books, 1979.

Saxton, Alexander P. *Indispensable Enemy: Labor and the Anti-Chinese Movement in California*. Berkeley and Los Angeles: University of California Press, 1971.

Taft, Philip. *The AF of L From the Death of Gompers to the Merger.* New York: Harper & Row, 1959.

Tess, John. *Uphill, Downhill, Yamhill: The Evolution of the Yamhill Historic District in Portland, Oregon.* Portland: Bureau of Planning, 1977.

Vaughan, Thomas, and Virginia Gates Ferriday, eds. *Space, Style and Structure: Building in the Pacific Northwest.* Portland: Oregon Historical Society, 1974.

ARTICLES

"Carpenters Local No. 1020 Honors Old-Time Members." *Oregon Carpenters' Yearbook.* Portland: Oregon State Council of Carpenters, 1964, p. 8.

"Pacific Coast Shipbuilding Agreement." *Monthly Labor Review* 54 (February 1942), p. 384.

"Recent Developments in Apprenticeship." *Monthly Labor Review* 69 (August 1949), pp. 126-30.

"Seasonality in Construction: A Continuing Problem." *Monthly Labor Review* 92 (December 1969), pp. 3-8.

"Structure of the Residential Building Industry, 1949." *Monthly Labor Review* 73 (October 1951), pp. 456-58.

"When Figures Lie." *Business Week*, 25 January 1947, pp. 32-34.

"Working Agreement for West Coast Shipbuilding Industry." *Monthly Labor Review* 63 (May 1941), pp. 1162-64.

Ankeny, George. "Local No. 583." *Oregon Carpenters' Yearbook.* Portland: Oregon State District Council of Carpenters, 1963, unpaginated.

Baker, Miner H. "Economic Growth Patterns in Washington and Oregon." *Monthly Labor Review* 82 (May 1959), pp. 502-508.

Bernstein, Irving. "Trade Union Characteristics, Membership, and Influence." *Monthly Labor Review* 82 (May 1959), pp. 530-35.

Dana, John. "Bargaining in the Western Lumber Industry." *Monthly Labor Review* 88 (August 1965), pp. 925-32.

Gordon, Margaret S. "Immigration and its Effect on Labor Force Characteristics." *Monthly Labor Review* 82 (May 1959), pp. 492-501.

Hogg, Thomas. "Negroes and Their Institutions in Oregon." *Phylon* 30 (Fall 1969), p. 285.

Kennedy, Van Dusen. "Association Bargaining." *Monthly Labor Review* 82 (May 1959), pp. 539-42.

Kerr, Clark. "West Coast Labor: Its Past and Its Prospects." *Monthly Labor Review* 82 (May 1959), pp. 489-91.

Krutsinger, Karl. "Apprenticeship Training Is Reported Lacking." *Oregon Carpenters' Yearbook*. Portland: Oregon State Council of Carpenters, 1963, p. 59.

Marshall, William A. "Workmen's Compensation Law: Notes on the Beginning." *Oregon Historical Quarterly* 54 (December 1953), pp. 273-90.

Personick, Martin E. "Union and Non-Union Pay Patterns in Construction." *Monthly Labor Review* 97 (August 1974), pp. 71-75.

Pierson, Frank C. "Building-Trades Bargaining Plan in Southern California." *Monthly Labor Review* 70 (January 1950), pp. 14-18.

Pollard, Lancaster. "The Pacific Northwest: A Regional Study." *Oregon Historical Quarterly* 52 (December 1951), pp. 211-34.

Reder, M.W. "Trends in Wages, Earnings, and Per Capita Income." *Monthly Labor Review* 82 (May 1959), pp. 524-29.

Ross, Arthur M. "Major Trends in Labor Relations." *Monthly Labor Review* 82 (May 1959), pp. 536-38.

Russell, Joe L., and Michael J. Pilot. "Seasonality in Construction: A Continuing Problem." *Monthly Labor Review* 92 (December 1969), pp. 3-8.

Schwantes, Carlos. "Protest in a Promised Land: Unemployment, Disinheritance, and the Origin of Labor Militancy in the Pacific Northwest, 1885-1886." *Western Historical Quarterly* 13 (October 1982), pp. 373-90.

Sleeman, B.W. "Retired Brother Reports on 56 Years of Service to UBCJA." *Oregon Carpenters' Yearbook*. Portland: Oregon State Council of Carpenters, 1962, p. 77.

Stone, Harry W. "Beginning of Labor Movement in the Pacific Northwest." *Oregon Historical Quarterly* 47 (January 1946), pp. 155-64.

Taft, Philip. "A Labor Historian Views Changes in the Trade Union Movement." *Monthly Labor Review* 92 (September 1969), pp. 8-11.

Tobie, Harry E. "Oregon Labor Disputes, 1919-23: I, The Living Wage." *Oregon Historical Quarterly* 48 (March 1947), pp. 7-24.

Weinberg, Edgar. "Reducing Skill Shortages in Construction." *Monthly Labor Review* 92 (February 1969), pp. 3-9.

THESES, DISSERTATIONS,
AND OTHER MANUSCRIPTS

Hoskins, Omar. "Some Aspects of Oregon Labor Organization From 1853 to 1902." Bachelor's thesis, Reed College, Portland, 1935.

Rydell, Robert W. "All the World's a Fair." Ph.D. dissertation, University of California, Los Angeles, 1982.

Triplett, Jack. "History of the Oregon Labor Movement Prior to the New Deal." Master's thesis, University of California, Berkeley, 1961.

"The *Oregonian* on the Labor Movement" [by Edith Feldman]. Portland. Oregon Historical Society. Archives.

Governmental Research Service. 1981. *Should The Federal Government Significantly Control the Powers of Labor Unions in the United States?* Washington, D.C.: U.S. Government Printing Office.

NEWSPAPERS AND PERIODICALS

Business Week

The Carpenter

Daily Journal of Commerce

Oregonian

Oregon Journal

Oregon Labor Press

Portland Labor Press

226 Reporter

Wall Street Journal

REPORTS AND DOCUMENTS AND GOVERNMENT PUBLICATIONS

"Master Labor Agreement." Union Contractors Association, 1983. Files of Local No. 247.

Minutes. Association for Building and Construction. 25 November 1922. Files of Local No. 247.

Minutes. Association for Building and Construction. 17 October 1922. Files of Local No. 247.

"Modifications to the Master Labor Agreement Between the Oregon-Columbia Chapter, the Associated General Contractors of America, Inc., and Oregon State District Council of Carpenters, UBCJA, and Southwest Washington District Council UBCJA." 8 February 1983. Files of the State District Council of Carpenters, Portland.

Packet from the Oregon State District Council of Carpenters, Third Annual Meeting, Hilton Hotel, Portland, Oregon. 25-27 April 1983. Files of the State District Council of Carpenters, Portland.

"Preliminary Proposal, Construction Industry Joint Labor-Management Cooperation Committee." 1982. In the files of the State District Council of Carpenters, Portland.

Press release from the office of Senator Robert Packwood. 23 August 1983. Files of the State District Council of Carpenters, Portland.

Press release from the office of the Oregon State District Council of Carpenters, 23 August 1983.

"Report on the Negro in Portland: A Progress Report, 1945-1957." *Portland City Club Bulletin* 37 (19 April 1957), pp. 355-70.

Ship Construction: Eight Selected West Coast Yards, 1941-1945. Washington, D.C.: U.S. War Manpower Commission, 1943. Archives of the Oregon Historical Society.

A Survey of Shipyard Operations in the Portland, Oregon Metropolitan Area. Washington, D.C.: U.S. War Manpower Commission, 1943. Archives of the Oregon Historical Society.

Twenty-First Annual Report of the Commissioner of Labor, 1906: Strikes and Lockouts. Washington, D.C.: U.S. Government Printing Office, 1907.

Anderson, Gust. Papers. Archives of the Oregon Historical Society.

Emergency Fleet Corporation. *Shipyard Occupations*. Philadelphia: U.S. Shipping Board, 1918. Archives of the Oregon Historical Society.

Loe, Kelly, ed. *Convention Proceedings of the Oregon State Federation of Labor for the Years 1902, 1903, 1904, 1905, 1907*. Portland: Oregon State Federation of Labor, 1928. Archives of the Oregon Historical Society.

U.S. Bureau of the Census. *Historical Statistics of the United States, Colonial Times to 1970*, Bicentennial ed. Washington, D.C., 1980.

U.S. Bureau of the Census. *Statistical Abstract of the United States*. 103rd ed. Washington, D.C., 1980.

CORRESPONDENCE

Ray Broughton to author, 13 April 1983.

David Johnson to author, 6 April 1983.

Joe Lane to Leo Larsen, 15 April 1983.

INTERVIEWS

Kate Barrett, 20 September 1984.

Clarence Blakeley, 28 June 1983.

Ray Broughton, 14 April 1983.

Harry Carlson, 22 February 1983.

————, and Dudley Franco, 9 February 1983.

Roy Coles, 19 July 1984.

George Edwards, 30 July 1983.

Dudley Franco, 4 March 1983.

Mark Furman, 23 August 1984.

Norman Garniere, 28 June 1983.

Carl Hiller, 11 September 1981.

Ed Olsen, 12 May 1983.

Andrew Sears, 17 September 1981.

Joe Stanley, 10 June 1983.

Fred I. Weber, Jr., 18 September 1984.

Art Wickstrand, 11 September 1981.

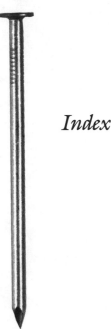

Index

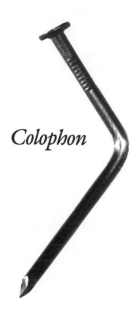

Colophon

The typeface used for display and text in *The City Build-ers* is ITC Galliard, designed by Matthew Carter. In 1986, Carter won the Frederic W. Goudy award for contributions to the printing industry. Typesetting was done by Irish Setter of Portland, Oregon. Printing and binding were performed by Thomson-Shore, Inc., of Dexter, Michigan, on 60-lb. Glatfelter paper.

The photographs of the nails on the title page and throughout this book were made by Strode Eckert Photographic of Portland, Oregon.

This book was designed and produced by the Oregon Historical Society Press.